The Trigger

Dr. Timothy Dosemagen

Bloomington, IN      Milton Keynes, UK

authorHOUSE™

AuthorHouse™
1663 Liberty Drive,
Suite 200
Bloomington, IN 47403
www.authorhouse.com
Phone: 1-800-839-8640

AuthorHouse™ UK Ltd.
500 Avebury Boulevard
Central Milton Keynes,
MK9 2BE
www.authorhouse.co.uk
Phone: 08001974150

First published by AuthorHouse 5/2/2006

ISBN: 1-4259-1876-X (sc)

Printed in the United States of America
Bloomington, Indiana

This book is printed on acid-free paper.

Other works by Dr. Dosemagen:
"Prodigies" (1stBooks, 2003)
"The Impossible" (AuthorHouse, 2004)

Table of Contents

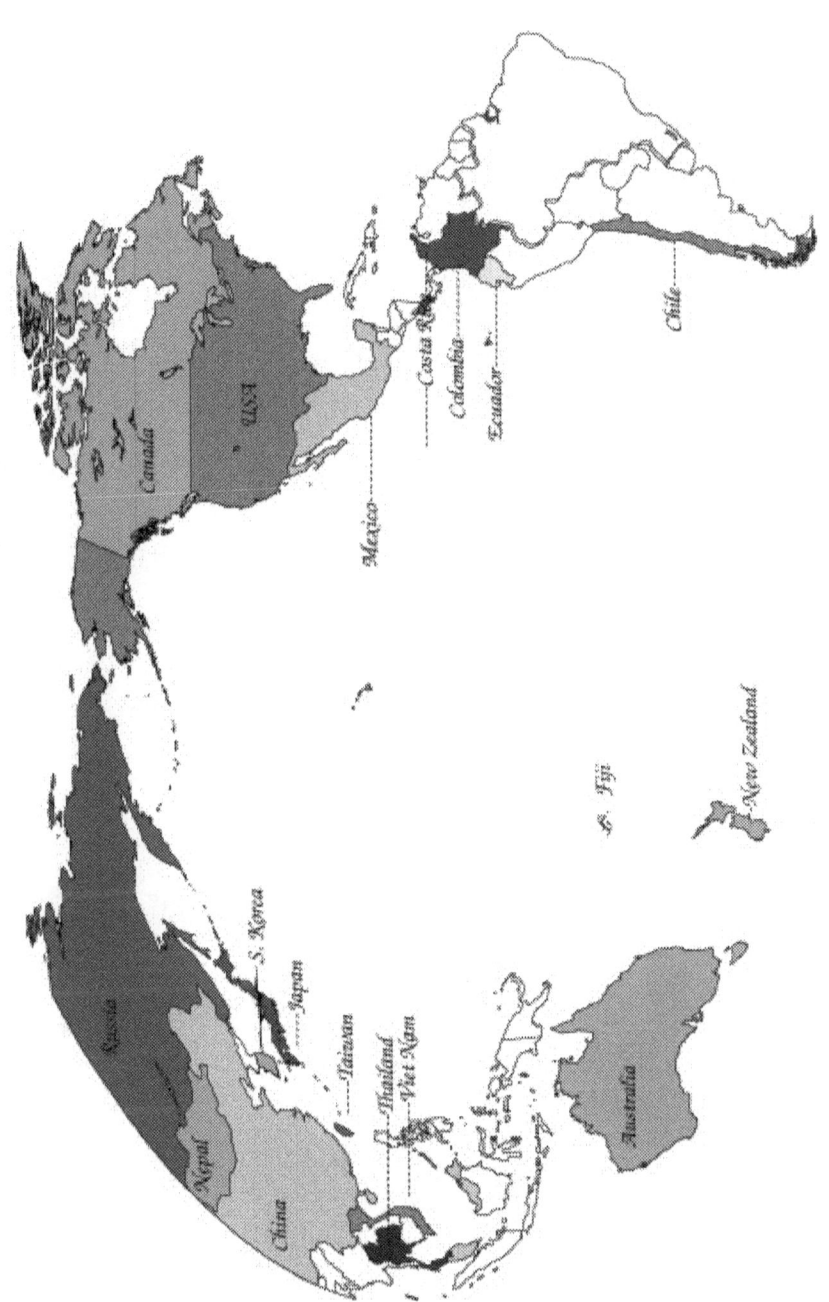

Prologue

While studying at the University of Maryland in the mid-1980s, in pursuit of my bachelors degree in Chinese Studies, I enrolled in a class on East-Asian politics, led by Dr. Dennis Doolin, former Under-Secretary of Defense for East-Asian Affairs under Melvin Laird, during the Nixon Administration. Doolin was a fantastic professor, and knew the region like the back of his hand.

Said Doolin, in words so prescient that I have never forgotten them, "I believe that in very short order, China will be our greatest challenger."

This was pretty difficult stuff to swallow, especially in the days of a China with $200 per capita incomes, an air force of Mig-19s, a small coastal defense navy, and in spite of a few years of post-Mao reforms, little in the way of economic innovation.

He went on. "I also believe that as long as things are going well for the Chinese, we have little to worry about. I'm concerned about what the Chinese would do after their first hard recession, or, God forbid, a depression."

"What do you think would happen?" I queried.

"Think only of Germany in the early 20th Century, and remember these truths. A great people will not stay down for long. A crowded nation will look for living space, and will take it by force. Nothing causes mischief more than totalitarian regimes in search for scapegoats," he replied.

Since that time, along with the rest of the world, I've watched, dumbstruck and amazed, at the rapid rise of China. Lecturing in Beijing back in 2004, I remember looking out over the city skyline and seeing dozens of cranes erecting skyscrapers. The scene was much the same in Shanghai back in 2002, where I was doing work with the Chinese Ministry of Education and the American International Education Foundation, paving the way for more Chinese students to study abroad in the United States.

All this time, I've often wondered what would happen if events forced the Chinese government to maintain stability and hold on to power by, in effect, "going crazy," much had once the German people.

Regional Snapshot: East Asia

Truth be known, everybody agreed that China was a rising power, but as the early years of the 21st Century dawned, she was barely a land power, at best. In fact, even today, China remains the only nation on earth capable of putting guns in the hands of 200 million fighters, and marching that army, which isn't too far a stretch when you consider that China's population is 1,300 millions. But that's a story for another, colder day.

East Asia is a tinderbox. As a region, it represents a unique crossroads, site of the world's densest juxtapositions of high stakes competition. To live in East Asia, as I have for no less than three years, is to dwell in a vibrant neighborhood of rising military and economic powers.

To look eastward toward the sunrise is to behold the most established regional power in mighty Japan, dominating the region with its $4.4 trillion economy, the world's second largest, and all from an amazing population of just 125 million, largely found on five islands no bigger than Montana. The Doomsday scenario has always been a Japan that decides to go nuclear, reacting to the rising North Korean threat, junking the Douglas MacArthur imposed Peace Constitution, once again choosing to exercise its right to impose its own will.

To look westward is to spy a waking China, the region's indisputable 'comer', with a population of 1.3 billion living in an area roughly equal to the U.S., east of the Mississippi. If all we leave behind are genes and ideas, the Chinese certainly are succeeding. China's economy, currently one third the size of the world's reigning colossus in the U.S.'s $12 trillion monster, is rising so rapidly, that it is projected to eclipse that of the U.S. by 2032. In 2005, China enjoyed a single year balance of trade surplus with the United States of nearly $200 billion dollars. In places like L.A., where if you listen very closely, you can actually hear the sucking sound from this historic, unprecedented bilateral transfer of wealth.

To see it taking place is even more remarkable, standing on the docks of Long Beach, on Los Angeles' southwestern elbow. All day long the mega-ships glide in, slowly but continuously floating in on peaceful blue waters, with the crate loaders swinging back and forth like metronomes, the ships slowly rising as they offload shipping crates filled with every product imaginable, fueling the voracious appetites of the greatest consuming classes of the world, in its largest market.

Following in the wake of these vessels as they return westward, like clockwork, an electronic torrent of dollars shoot through cyberspace, desperately keeping the ships coming in, at the amazing pace of $7,000 per second, a $200 billion annual surplus that finances China's sparkling new cities and gleaming factories and rising middle classes and their fancy new toys.

Look to the north and behold Russia's tremendously rich Siberian / Pacific region, with its huge reserves of oil, metals, water, timber and living space. History forgets that in the mid-1800s when Qing Dynasty China was weak and Tsarist Russia was strong, Russia stole two California-sized pieces of real estate from China's Siberian / Pacific flank via the treaties of Nerchinsk and Amur. China has not forgotten, and as a crowded, rising power finding herself increasingly thirsty for oil and land, Russia can only watch as its potential opponent slowly, patiently adds pieces to a leveling chessboard.

In the center of this economic maelstrom stands Korea. The Ireland of Asia, an ancient nation of poets and fast friendships, as well as millennia of enduring the bullying of larger powers, Korea, also known as The Land of Morning Calm, once again finds herself temporarily divided. Korea is at the center of it all. During the opening years of the Global War On Terror, some in Washington actually had the temerity to suggest that the United States actually invade North Korea. What an impossible imperial dream that was.

South Korea, rising from the ashes in 1953, is a constitutional republic with the world's 11th largest economy, sitting on a land area roughly the size of Indiana, with a busy population of 46 million. Long suspected of having its own nuclear weapons (aside from the U.S. umbrella) it is the most wired nation state on earth, with near saturation in per capita use of cell phones and the Internet, enjoying a summer monsoon and warm ocean currents that produce rich rice crops. If the Koreas ever merged, they would rapidly rival their former imperial masters in Japan in nearly every measurable category. A united Korea would also cause great discomfort to Korea's western neighbors. The Middle-Kingdom, after all, has always demanded loyalty from its client states.

The North, slightly larger in area and organized into a people's republic, slogs a basket case economy yielding annual food and fuel shortages for its 20 million citizens, beset by extended droughts on colder, less fertile land, and led by a paranoid, totalitarian Confucian-Stalinist communist model. Created in the Chinese image and defended to the death by one million Chinese, after insulted U.S. forces marched north to the Yalu in reply to the naked Northern aggression of June, 1950, North Korea scratched its way to the acquisition of nuclear weapons, with plenty of long-range Taepodong missiles to carry them. Japan, home to the U.S. Navy's 7th Fleet, tolerates these weapons only because it currently can, under the cool shade of the U.S. nuclear umbrella.

Once, back in the 1990s, the North actually shot one of these Taepodong missiles eastward over the Japanese mainland, startling the sleeping Nipponese. These Taepodong missiles (and the nukes they can carry) mean big time cash for the North. Imagine what Bin Laden or some other of the world's failures would pay to get just one, slipping it deep into one of the Great Satan's ports, perhaps on one of those 17 million cargo containers now plying the seas, bearing names like Han Jin, COSCO, Maersk, Evergreen, Honda or China Cargo.

In 1946, at the end of its Imperial Japanese occupation of 100 years and preceded by centuries of suzerainty to various Chinese regimes, a united Korea finally stood at the brink of fair competition with both a newly defeated Japan, and a Nationalist China at civil war with communist insurgents. Tragically, this window of opportunity was to close after only three trying years of attempted politicization, rebuilding, de-Japanization, long lines and influence peddling.

Most tragically for the Koreans, the power vacuum was rapidly filled by Russia, which established its zone of influence north of the 38th parallel, and then by the United States, which set up its power base in the south. The North, in a power grab that attempted to redress the unfair and imposed allocation of Korea's northern natural resources, separate from its southern agricultural base, launched a vicious three year war before elections could democratize the South, leaving more than 5 million Koreans, a million Chinese, and 35,000 Americans dead. Although The North's aggression was finally fought to a draw, the division of the peninsula still insults the Koreans more than half a century after the war.

It is precisely this juxtaposition of military, economic and political interests that makes the Koreas East Asia's (and the world's) highest stakes flashpoint. In geopolitical terms, to borrow a phrase from Southern California lexicon, Korea is 'The Big One'. The question has always been when, not if.

In raw power, the military interests of the three most powerful nations on earth, Russia, China and The United States, grind against each other in Korea. China, now possessing 500 nuclear weapons, is rapidly expanding the capabilities of its historically coastal defense navy with ballistic missile submarines, and is presently laying keel on a homemade aircraft carrier, after purchasing another from Spain in 1996.

There is only one reason for aircraft carriers, and that is power projection. The Chinese are learning what the U.S. and Japan learned in places like the Coral Sea and Midway. Now seeking to leapfrog into space-based weaponry, the Chinese insist on protecting the interests of North Korea, dreaming of the day (it will come) when the American footprint will at last leave East Asia, returning the region to its historic equilibrium, with China at the center. The Korean peninsula is key to this strategy.

Russia, with 20,000 nuclear weapons and a post-Communist economy roughly equal to that of Holland, is like a muscle-bound farmer with mounds of debt, an abundance of land, and a proud population of 140,000,000. With its equally proud history of growth, ambition and survival, as well as a growing reliance on oil exports to balance its federal budget, all of these factors combine to produce in Russia the most powerful, unstable nation state on earth.

The Russians insist on supporting a separate North Korea, while recognizing their own shifting power relationship with China, and growing dependence on Japan and the United States. Hoping to use its new relationship with The West in a triangulated game of chess, holding the Chinese to their present position for as long as possible, Russia nervously covets the rapid economic growth of the region, seeking the same for its huge Siberian and East Asian landmass. For Russia, the American presence in Korea is the vital key to keeping the Chinese at bay, and the Americans in play.

The United States, with its $440 billion annual defense expenditures and Global War On Terror burdens, has long planned the full withdrawal of its 35,000 troops from South Korea. Can it be any different for America in light of her $.5 trillion annual budget deficits and a $8 trillion National Debt? This shift in power makes the Japanese and Russians extremely nervous as they eye the Chinese, and such a move, proposed as recently as during the Carter Administration, promises untold aftershocks beyond the 38th parallel. Which brings our story back to the very center of the bull's-eye: Korea.

The North has several nuclear weapons, a desperate need for cash, annual famines, and a standing army of 1,000,000. The South, with its U.S. nuclear umbrella, powerful economy and 600,000 strong military, sits on the world's last remaining fully cocked trigger for World War Three: 35,000 American G.I.s. If the North ever attacks, those young men and women are goners, and Washington, Beijing, Moscow, Tokyo, Pyongyang and Seoul all know it. But remember, those G.I.s are just a trigger – just enough of a presence to guarantee the righteous unleashing of Yankee hell.

From The Roman Empire Until The British Empire: On China & Being #1

Sometime during the reign of the first Roman Emperors in the 1st Century A.D., the economy of Rome eclipsed that of China. This economic supremacy continued for several centuries, and subsequent world economic leadership fell back to China, with also-rans spread amongst the European powers, drifting from Russia to Spain, from Holland to Italy, to the Holy Roman Empire, and from France finally to England, with her growing Empire. For nearly 13 centuries, China had been the number one economic power in the world.

Spain, Holland and Britain ruled the 16th Century, with Britain leading the way through the 17th and 18th Centuries, finally being replaced by the United States from the late 19th through the early 21st Century. China, with her 1,300 millions of people and rapidly growing economy, was projected to overcome the U.S. as number one by the year 2032.

In the year 2010, the top five economies of the world, in gross domestic product, stood as follows:

#1: United States:.	$12.5 trillion
#2: Japan: . .	$5 trillion
#3: China: . .	$3.8 trillion
#4: Germany: .	$3.6 trillion
#5: United Kingdom:	$3.3 trillion

But economic power is a much more complex equation than simply measuring GDP. Subtracting from economic power are other factors, such as reliance on imported raw materials, national debt, negative balance of trade, and low currency valuations.

Adding to economic power are cash holdings, direct foreign investment, control over raw material supplies, acting as a source of essential materials, and a highly prized currency.

By 2010, China had amassed huge cash reserves, and owned over 10% of the United States' national debt outright. Growing crude oil import supply chains were being rapidly diverted from the Middle East to Siberia, the Yuan was rising in value, and annual balance of trade surpluses were approaching half a trillion dollars. China was growing richer, stronger, and more self reliant.

By 2010, the United States had amassed a national debt nearly two thirds the size of its mammoth economy, was importing over half of its crude oil, largely via the Middle-East through vulnerable sea shipping lanes, it dollar was falling in value, and it was running over 750 billion dollars in annual trade deficits.

Battle Of The Super Languages
– The Torch Is Passed

Language is power.

Even the most casual observer could see the growing competition between China and the United States, especially in the opening years of the 21st Century, at the dawn of the Information Age. The battle was being fought by the users of language for the control of information and wealth, and the domination of whole industries.

In the Information Age, no one will deny that language, no matter how diverse, is the common denominator of information, making language the key ingredient of our times. Language is living information, it is through words that information is gathered, coded, logged, and hopefully passed down the human chain. Until telepathy is widely developed, or until that Golden Day that pure empathic intelligence becomes the norm for our species, or perhaps until the day when the images eclipse words, for better or for worse, language is the only hope we have for continuing the ongoing exchange of information.

In this respect, civilization depends on the exchange of language. Therefore, the better this exchange functions, the more perfect our world becomes, and the better our civilization functions. Even so, for the time being at least, the world's exchange of information is flawed. Modernization has brought us ever closer together, but despite the jelling of neighborhood earth, our unnecessary surplus of languages keeps us apart. In the world community of the Information Age, the 'foreign' language is rapidly becoming an anachronism.

Then came the year 2000, when the pendulum swung, and the number of English language users of the Internet, for the first time, were exceeded by the number of Chinese users. The moment was historic, and noticed by many in the Chinese People's Republic. A new revolution beckoned, with a sparkling new battle cry: We the people, in order to form a more perfect world, with equal access to all information, demand one language for all: Chinese.

Suppose for a moment what kind of world this would be if all 7,000,000,000 of us agreed to transfer our information via the same code. Utopian visions of no misunderstandings between nations pop into mind, leaving distance, time and energy as the only remaining obstacles to the desegregation of neighborhood earth. (Assuming, of course, that utopia's citizenry has eliminated that other nagging source of segregation, this being prejudice.) Even unilingual earth will not be without its drawbacks – just think of all the unemployed translators, interpreters and language instructors. Alas, there are no true utopias.

All disadvantages aside, the thought of a universal tongue in humankind's future causes great excitement. Then reality, unkind as it often is, returns us to our present day Tower of Babel world, teeming with hundreds of languages and thousands of dialects, all along under the constant squeeze and cruel vice of modernization. It is an illogical world indeed, but things are getting better as this new and wonderful Information Age matures. Today, for lack of better words (no pun intended) we are all witnessing the dawn of the Super Languages.

If necessity is truly the mother of invention, the Super Languages are growing out of the desperate need for interface in our rapidly connecting world. Among the chief contributors to this rise of the Super Languages are:

1. The unprecedented rise in international communications;
2. The growing wealth of China and the United States;
3. Recent waves of immigration;
4. The not so innocent bouts of nation taming being undertaken by the Colonial or Hegemonic Powers.

While the evils of Colonialism are well founded, all observers must admit that English has been particularly well served, uniquely blessed by fate in that its driving forces, Great

Britain (Colonialism) and the United States (Hegemonism) worked to propel the language much like the first and second stages of a rocket, driving onward and outward the push of the language throughout the world and beyond. To continue using our metaphor, the third stage of the rocket is the Internet, particularly global commerce and e-education.

Lest anyone doubt the universality of English, this language is currently being used by an estimated quarter of the earth's inhabitants as either mother tongue, or much more often, as a second, third, or even fourth language. Ask any Brit, Yank, Aussie or Kiwi – when traveling abroad, how often is one met by foreigners who, for one reason or another, (usually economic) speak Super Language English, oftentimes better than the Super Language native speakers themselves.

At the dawn of the 21st Century, another Super Language is being passed around the streets of neighborhood earth, one that has already quietly passed by English in gross Internet users, and one with the potential to overtake English as the most commonly used language on earth: Chinese.

Make no mistake – the Chinese language, by sheer weight of numbers, is already a card carrying member of the exclusive club of Super Languages. Chinese Mandarin now boasts in excess of one billion native, primary language speakers, easily surpassing English as the dominant native language. Chinese is a language that intrigues, due not only to its growing popularity, but also by way of its logic, and most significantly through its beautiful links with the past offered via its written form, the 3,000 or so (required to read newspapers) characters.

Such a language as this deserves closer scrutiny. What is Chinese? What effects does this language have upon its users? Where did Chinese come from? What's so special about Chinese?

In so far as the transfer of information goes, Chinese is actually no more efficient than its counterpart in Club Super Language. In essence, it is a structured gathering of mono-syllabic bits and pieces which, when thrown together in varying combinations, takes on the intended meanings of it users.

Actually, Chinese is similar to English in several respects, but with respect to grammar, Chinese far surpasses English in its simplicity. Chinese also requires the memorization of far fewer words to achieve fluency, has far fewer words to choose from, and borrows far less from other languages.

The key distinction between Chinese and English lies in its written form, which is both unique in its unbroken evolution, and instrumental in the world outlook within which it so subtly inculcates its users.

The Chinese script is ancient. Written forms of contemporary characters have been dated back in time as far as the 16th Century B.C. In an effort to see into the future, Shang Dynasty soothsayers meticulously inscribed crude drawings (pictograms) representing objects, time markers and feelings onto the bones (most often the scapula) of animals. Once these pictograms were so inscribed, the bones were subject to the heat of the fire ring, then cooled by being thrown into a cold bucket of water, resulting in the formation of cracks on the surface of the bones, which thus connected the characters into trails of communication. Seers then carefully analyzed the cracked surfaces of the bones (and their messages) for the purpose of fortune telling, leading toward the modern script that we now find splayed across countless menus across the globe today.

We can see how the search for the future led the ancient Chinese directly to it, in a beautifully woven evolutionary strand that remains unbroken through to the present time. To understand this unique quality is to appreciate what it is to be Chinese.

Amazingly, many of the pictograms used by the ancients to tell fortunes some 3,500 years ago are still in use today, in a modernized form. What's even more amazing is that, to this day, Chinese high school students can read, and to some degree comprehend the messages as written by their ancestors three and one-half millennia ago.

These valuable links to the past are not to be underestimated. As an American, 3,500 years from now, I wonder what will remain of my culture, uniting me with my progeny. The values of freedoms? The values of wealth accumulation and the pursuit of happiness? English and American literature? Highways, stadiums and public works? No need to wonder in East Asia.

To become literate in modern Chinese, students suffer through years of rote memorization involving the history of each character, its source, the manner in which the character is drawn and painted, its individual meanings, its combined meanings, and its nuances. Learn 3,000 or so of these pictograms (characters) and you have achieved literacy. Modern day Chinese scholars can approach an understanding of over 10,000 individual characters, some of these pictograms exceeding 20 brush strokes in their rendering. Needless to say, the Chinese language is an art form, it is slowly acquired, and must be painstakingly learned. But unlike English, the language actually makes sense.

English speakers, in their ignorance (or arrogance) often query, "Why haven't the Chinese streamlined the learning process of these time consuming characters into an alphabet?" After all, the Koreans and the Japanese did so!

Someday it might happen – but let's hope that whenever it does, the Chinese skip the baggage of English-styled alphabets, with all their inherent problems of too many letters with the same sounds, or too many nearly identical letters, or the entire crazy spelling dysfunction which so defines English as a language, frustrating English as a second language learners, mostly the modern Latinate words such as 'tableaux' or 'prophylactic'.

Aside from Chinese resistance and cultural pride, one possible answer as to why alphabetization hasn't yet happened to Chinese lies within the complexity of the language. A number of alphabets have been created in attempts to Romanize Chinese. The latest evolution of this movement, called Pinyin, was formally instituted by the Communists in the 1960s, giving the Western Mind (and Press) the added challenge of distinguishing between 'Peiping' and 'Beijing'. For instance, 'Teng Hsiao Ping' was slimmed down to the current 'Deng Xiao

Ping', and 'Hsinhwa' (a news service) was liposuctioned into the much more svelte and certainly easier 'Xinhua'.

Despite government efforts to the contrary, these alphabets have never caught on in China. The root of the problem lies in the common pronunciations of so many of the various pictograms. Imagine a language where 12 words with 12 different meanings are all alphabetized alike, with the same Romanizations, but different pictograms? For example, the Pinyinized Chinese sentence, "Ma ma ma ma ma?" when translated into English, might read, "Did Mother scold the horse?"

Although a consideration of context and the application of tones can have an ameliorating effect on the confusions inherent in written Chinese, the Chinese people continue to simply avoid any confusion by choosing pictograms over alphabets. Bravo to the Chinese! - for as we shall see, the troubles endured in the writing of Chinese are not without their rewards.

English, to be sure, has its own merits. It is by far the more pliant of the two Super Languages, able to adapt quickly to new technologies and demands, a fact that in no small degree is reflected in the current traits of its best users. Chinese, while more logical and less grammatically complex, is a more cumbersome giant – old and proud, not as quick to adapt, again, (at least before 1979) somewhat indicative of its users.

No question, for the practitioner of Modern Chinese, the description of new technologies is particularly difficult. For example, the Chinese characters for 'movie' or 'motion picture' are, literally, 'electric shadow'. Other new arrivals on the technological stage are simply transliterated or mimicked, as is the case with the word 'Kevlar', which is a new composite armor used in modern tanks, or helmets. The Chinese write, 'Ke Fu La', a sound imitation of the original word. The writer once spent hours looking for the new word in an older dictionary, all the while querying contemporary Chinese on what the substance could possibly be, to no avail. This is a developing trend.

But it remains arguable that the historical influences and ties which a given language provides its users either consciously or sub-consciously affects the ways in which they gather information, rationalize it, reason with it, and choose to act on it at any given moment in time. Each Super Language has unique ties to the past.

While the merits of Chinese and English are self evident, let us not forget that the Chinese language has the added advantages of offering its users sorely needed historical ties, indeed, cultural anchors, as its users brace for the quickening storm of The Information Age, awash in a sea of information and images. Advanced or backwards, rich or poor, all of the earth's language users share one common tie: we are equally caught up in this race, call it what you may - modernization, or globalization, or internationalization.

Doubters reading this article need only glimpse the speed of change by viewing the now famous photos of the earth as viewed from space after dark. The brighter the lights, the faster the pace of change - enter the Super Languages.

Some will weather this storm better than others, forging ahead faster at times, with very much dependent upon the perspectives a nation has, both materialistic and historic, ultimately affecting that nation's self-image. In the prior two centuries, English has been the premier language of discovery, the mother tongue of great inventions and discoveries. English rides the many probes racing their way into deep space. English sits inscribed atop most of the earth-sourced leftovers on our moon, on Venus, on Mars, and on Saturn's moon Titan.

Lest we speakers of English rest for too long on our laurels, a billion Chinese speakers, 700,000,000 Hindi speakers, 300,000,000 Spanish speakers, 140,000,000 Russian speakers, 125,000,000 Japanese speakers, 90 million German speakers, 80 million Vietnamese speakers and 70 million Korean speakers are at our side in this grand race, holding up the mirror for us, adding new words to our lexicon, like the growing electioneering buzzword "Competitiveness". So dominant is English that those international laggards, the French, now find themselves in the reactionary mode of defending their mother tongue from elimination by English with legislation, not only in France, but Quebec.

Yet, the dangers of running too far too fast in this linguistic evolution are apparent. Present technological omens notwithstanding (Three Mile Island, Chernobyl) we must remember that people, when faced with the rapid eradication of the most salient feature of their culture, dig in and react, often violently. These failures of the earth often act out by using terror (Radical Islam) when they feel overwhelmed by historic momentum.

As Americans, we fancy ourselves in the lead in this race, but as the 21st Century dawns, such assumptions are no longer quite as valid. We Americans like to think that we know where we come from, but as our ties to the past are continually rejected in the rush to embrace modernization, do we really have any idea? The family, that time-tested bastion of ancient ties, is now an endangered American species, in an age of 35% single parent families, and 50% divorce rates.

Substitute the late night television admonition of "It's 12:00. Parents, do you know where your children are?" With "It's 2010 – children, do you know where your parents are? Do you know where your ancestors come from? Do you know what your family is about?" To answer these (and many deeper questions) indeed, to find the American place in lasting history, we must view ourselves relative to the people who have endured. Is it a coincidence that the Chinese, with their Super Language as an anchor, have endured as no others, maintaining their links to the past?

All we leave behind in this world are genes and ideas. There are 1,300 millions Chinese living in China. There are 340 millions overseas Chinese, more than the population of the United States and Canada. That's significant.

So too is the dominance of ideas from the Western mind, primarily English speaking. But remember, ideas can be translated.

The other Super Language, Chinese, is as old as civilization, and yet as noisy and vibrant as any language around, and still growing. Each Chinese pictogram is a story passed down through the ages, told and retold, altered here and there, yet always joining the current users with the ancient family. Each character is an ancient photograph taken by the eye of mankind, developed in the minds of the users, reproduced again and again by the hands of the people, over the eons, never fading, never crumbling, never getting lost from the photo album, fresh as the new meanings to be conveyed.

Each word is a museum, visited daily by the Chinese, a relic of history passed along to the future, to help in the race through the storm. What better anchor for the present?

Perhaps it was good that we Americans didn't take the time to appreciate the links to our past which our own Super Language provided. As we glided through the present, racing onward and outward like an orphaned child, we continued to discover first, we continued to be the first to learn, reassured by nothing more (or less) than our faith in God, as we knocked on his many doors.

Then came the year 2000, when the pendulum swung, and the number of English language users of the Internet, for the first time, were exceeded by the number of Chinese users. The moment was historic, yet noticed by few in the United States.

The Chinese noticed.

Olympic Afterglow

The 2008 Summer Games in Beijing had come off so well, the results went beyond even the wildest imaginings of the most ambitious Chinese. China had finally arrived in so many ways, not the least of which was the final medals count, which placed China squarely atop the world, with not only the most medals overall, but the most Gold medals, and the most Bronze medals, of any nation, even besting their archrival the United States, which came in a very close second in the overall medals count, and politely acknowledged the home field.

It was a sea change, and a psychological master stroke for the hopes and aspirations of the Third World, and all the rest of those nations long tired of U.S. domination of world sport. An old established balance of forces, going back at least to the Cold War, once held it that in any given Olympics, you could count on the Russians to dominate in games of power and strength, for the Americans to control in games of speed and elegance, and for the Chinese to win in games of precision and accuracy. This basic formula had held steady all the way from between the World Wars through the 2004 Summer Games in Athens.

That all changed in Beijing in 2008, and on judgment after judgment, close call after close call, the Chinese just seemed to keep coming out on top. Some attributed it to officiating that had been pre-arranged, or to the home field advantage of bias in judging, or crowd noise, or the desire to be polite to the host nation – and hadn't the Chinese been ever so gracious hosts?

After all, China had been an unlikely choice for The Games, and these Olympics had been cast in a very artificial light since their inception, being staged to celebrate sport in a land where a quarter of the population lacked access to flush toilets, where the selection and cultivation of sports stars began at age 2, where the 'lucky' were sent far from home to join 'sports stables' with mandatory membership lasting the duration of childhood, or else the family benefits and other niceties would be immediately cut off. In China, producing sport prowess was akin to economic production, not unlike the old Eastern-Bloc of Cold War days.

Strangest of all, because of China's horrific air pollution problem, Beijing being the most air polluted city on earth, to stage the games, the entire industrial production of northern China eerily had to be shut down, beginning 5 days before the games, and augmented by a temporary ban on home coal burning, the preferred method of heating on the cool nights.

The effects were both artificial and immediate - Beijingers, long used to counting 'Blue Sky Days' on one hand, marveled at the sight of constellations during the wonderfully clear evenings during the Olympics.

Less than 5 minutes after the end of the closing ceremonies, the factories reopened. Athletes with asthma immediately noticed the change, as did the throngs of tourists who lingered for a few days after the games, noticing a thin layer of white dust on their shoes, even after a walk of just a few blocks, and the yellowish hue of the midday sky, with the complete disappearance of the sun in a nightly pinkish haze, long before sunset.

But the afterglow of these games was less transient than that of a single sunset, or a clear evening sky. Indeed, these games had marked the arrival of a New China, one which could successfully stage world class events, winning them at the same time. China had finally retaken her lead in the arena of world sport – could economic and military prowess be far behind?

Chinese Political Philosophy

To most Chinese, Democracy is a wonderful invention that, if practicable, would make a nice import some day, but wouldn't presently work in modern China. Historically, in well over a dozen revolutions and new dynastic rulers, until the 20th Century, China had never known democracy. Then, during the 20th Century, after the overthrow of the corrupt Qing Dynasty, a new Chinese Republic, led by Dr. Sun Yat Sen, actually attempted a rapid installation of democratic practices. Sadly, decades of corruption, warlordism, a Japanese invasion, World War Two, and the rise of the Communists drove democracy off the Chinese mainland, where it slowly incubated and grew into the noisy, participative democracy known as the Republic of China, on Taiwan.

Taiwan, and its participative democracy, proved that the Chinese people could handle self rule, but the system threatened the Communists, and remained a thorn in Beijing's side, which demanded repatriation of the renegade province, which the United States long opposed. To the Communist Chinese apparatchik way of thinking, "You Americans have your Cuba, and we Chinese have our Taiwan."

Back on the mainland, the key to politics had always been to keep the masses contented, once having wrested power. Political stability has been the mantra of the Chinese Communists for four decades, especially as the population's means of communication were slowly unshackled and freed by the economic reforms begun in 1979 by Premier Deng Xiao Ping, and accelerated by the dawning of technologies such as the fax machine, the mobile telephone, and the Internet. The free sharing of information had been largely tolerated, if not welcomed, as long as it kept the masses focused on improving their economic lot in life, while keeping China Inc. growing in economic clout.

Occasionally, democratic movements rose up, either out of economic displacement (rising agricultural sector unemployment), or in protest of being physically moved to make way for massive engineering projects (Three Gorges Dam), out of religious persecution (Fa Lun Gong Movement), out of sheer frustration with the callousness of government incompetence (coal mine explosions, AIDS transmission through dirty needles, corruption), or youthful frustrations (Tian An Men Square). Each and every uprising was brutally suppressed, and with the exception of a rising tide of youthful free speakers, the population of China remained politically docile, and democracy was put off, again and again, on the wish list of a possibly brighter future.

The key was maintaining political stability at all costs, and anything that threatened the status quo, which meant control of the people by the government and for the government, was not acceptable.

Most East Asians viewed the United States as a newcomer, a 'Johnny come lately' to the historical parade of Superpowers, flush with recent successes, but burning the candle at both ends, and flaming out too rapidly for the betterment of long term global stability.

Most East Asians liked Americans. After the Second World War, for a few decades, there was even an awestricken admiration of the Americans and things Western, sometimes viewed through the fables of imported movies, or through the lens of a Life magazine, or perhaps through the stories of those who had occasion to travel to this fabled land of widespread wealth, or via a trip to Japan, which was doing its level best to copy the Yankees, matching their wealth, productivity, and even their prowess at the games of baseball and golf.

But for the Chinese, such feelings of affinity quickly disappeared during the Korean War, where no fewer than a million Chinese patriots lost their lives battling the Americans, helping their North Korean Communist brethren beat back the Yankees all the way from the Yalu to the 38th parallel. Then came the well known Yankee horror shows of complete exploitation of the Vietnamese people, with their drinking halls, gambling parlors, whorehouses, slave labor factories, aluminum mines and military posts dotting Southeast Asia, from the 17th parallel southward. It had taken no more than 10 years of armed struggle to oust the French, and 20 more years to jack up the Americans, sweeping their imperialist boot prints off of the Asian landmass by assisting their Communist Vietnamese brethren with skills in bomb making, insurrection, weaponry, and a slow infiltration of the wicked, stinking Western-styled military and government.

The coup de grace for any remaining respect the Chinese had for the Americans came after their economic growth began to take hold, and the Americans began borrowing a billion dollars a day to finance their excesses, keeping their insatiable appetites for foreign imports satiated by exporting increasingly useless dollars and governmental debt issuances.

The Communist Chinese despised these excesses, and called the malaise of too many freedoms a 'Spiritual Pollution,' both economic and social, in a land where homosexuality was adored, divorce was widely tolerated, dogs were pampered with fine food and manicures, religion was worn like a medal or carried like a cross, humility was uncool, tattoos, bling and consumption were conspicuous, and a going it alone, antisocial, superior attitude was the norm.

"It won't last," most Chinese would answer when asked about America's pre-eminence. "Amazing, and vulgar, and transient," was the majority opinion.

Puns On A 60ᵗʰ Birthday

Du Meigen, one of the best pure linguists ever produced by the National Security Agency of the United States, had been on operations somewhere in East Asia for at least three decades. He was referred to as an 'Old China Hand', a person of some trust in the interpretation of affairs Chinese, but Meigen knew better.

He had been awarded his name back in Taiwan in the early 1980s, a near transliteration of his Western name, three characters which each contained the Chinese radical for 'wood', or 'tree'. The person who adorned him with this odd name said that it made sense, after all, he was a tall, lanky, long-legged American, and hadn't he been born under the sign of the Wood Tiger? It made sense, and it stuck, and it was easier than trying to get Chinese to pronounce his real name, and after hearing the name spoken enough times, it made him feel as if he was actually assimilating into the overwhelming culture, but Meigen certainly knew better than to assume such impossibilities.

It was one thing to be able to hold a conversation in Chinese, and quite a special affair to be able to pick up and read a newspaper or magazine in the complicated script, requiring the memorization of at least 2,500 of the ancient Chinese pictograms. In fact, if one lived amongst the people long enough, absorbing oneself into the history of the culture, soaking in the sights, sounds, smells, tastes and feel of the place, after a very long time, one could actually begin falling victim to the cruel trick of feeling Chinese.

It was on one of these occasions, while off operations, that Meigen found himself invited to the 60ᵗʰ birthday party of a notable local politician. The Chinese zodiac is set up to follow 12 year cycles, and the completion of the 5ᵗʰ 12 year cycle was a very special event indeed, so turning 60 is a huge affair for reasons more significant than reaching a milestone in age, and must be celebrated by the eating of sumptuous food, fine and abundant drink, lively and sometimes bawdy entertainment, silly pranks, lots of good fun poking, and, of course, gifts.

During the latter stages of the affair, well beyond the sober shores of decorum and deep beyond the safe harbors of couth and rationality, the alcohol having taken command, Meigen found himself in the midst of a table game, where each person seated at the large round table was uttering two words, which usually evoked lots of laughter, so he assumed these were words that could be describing the guest of honor in a kind hearted, but playful way of poking fun.

Each time it came time for Meigen to say his words, he did his best to find the right turn of phrase, so as not to offend, yet to elicit a laugh, and stay in the game, after all, he was the only Westerner at the table and didn't want to appear 'square,' or 'different.' Each try seemed to work, eliciting a few laughs here, a few smiles there, along with some puzzled expressions. Laughing at the iterations of the others at the table was no problem at all, as after each round, more rounds of plum wine and beer were served. After a while, it seemed as if the entire table had the giggles, and the celebrants seemed happy.

Finally, the game ended, and as most of the celebrants departed for safe taxi rides home, one young lady grabbed Meigen's arm, intently asking him if he understood the game that had just been played. It was a silly question, of course he understood it, it was a funny game of poking fun with words, he meekly replied, trying to understand the query.

"No, those words were Chinese puns," said the young lady. "I thought you should know. I thought you played very well, most of the time," she added.

The strange feeling Meigen felt on the ride home from the party lasted for days, and then weeks, and then months. It was a feeling of recognition, of knowing that one could never completely crack this culture no matter how hard or how long one tried, that the state of being foreign was so strong here that it did no good to attempt to overcome it.

And from that day onward, Meigen remembered an important lesson one of his American instructors had told him long ago when he was studying how to report secret information using distance communications technology. "You will never completely blend into Asia," he said, "and don't ever be fooled into thinking you can, you're not bred for it, you don't look the part, and you haven't the time to master the nuances of the culture. If you want to try disappearing into a society, try going to East Germany, where you'd have a chance."

It was a lesson Meigen would never forget.

The Chinese Word For Money

To the Americans, the word for money was simply five alphabetic symbols that spelled out a rough concept. To the Chinese, their word for money was an ancient pictogram of gold, protected by a spear. For over 30 years, the Americans, through their modern financial alchemy of turning I.O.U.s into current wealth, had found a magical formula, allowing the nation's citizenry to live far beyond its means, through massive borrowing, largely from the rising East-Asian economies of China, Japan, Korea and Taiwan. After all, the Asians needed a place to park their wealth, and the Americans hadn't the discipline to balance their budgets.

In 1979, U.S. President James Earl Carter expressed horror at the fact that the National Debt of the United States was about to eclipse one trillion dollars. By the year 2010, U.S. National Debt had reached an astounding ten trillion dollars, nearly the size of its entire Gross National Product.

In 1979, Chinese Premier Deng Xiaoping declared that it was good to get rich, with Chinese per capita income standing at $150 per person. By the year 2010, 30 uninterrupted years of 9% annual economic growth had produced in the Chinese economy the world's third largest, at 4 trillion dollars, second only to those of Japan and the U.S.

During this amazing run of Chinese export-led growth, and American borrowing, the government-run, centrally planned Chinese economy invested heavily in U.S. treasury bonds. In effect, China fueled America's penchant for living beyond its means, purchasing its debt, allowing the U.S. to keep its interest rates artificially low, fueling The Great Stock Boom of the 1990s, and The Great Real Estate Boom of the 2000s, keeping the American appetite for Chinese exports strong. As China manufactured and sold, and as the U.S. borrowed and purchased, the Chinese government amassed over a trillion dollars in U.S. debt, in effect, owning 10% of the U.S.'s entire National Debt.

Many Chinese Dynasties had gone on borrowing binges in the past, and to Chinese sensibilities, the Americans were just hastening the end of their first great Dynastic Cycle. Over a dozen times in China's history, the nation had experienced revolution, followed by the establishment of a new government, followed by a period of solid governance, growth and expansion, followed by larger and greater government largesse and borrowing, greater taxation, taxpayer revolts, federal corruption, imperial overreach, and finally, revolution.

America was simply in the waning days of her first run as a world power, and to fuel her rise as a world power, the Chinese had simply chosen to invest in the engine of her export-led growth, in effect, like spiking a cow's diet with growth hormones, keeping the milk coming as quickly as inexpensively as possible, for the near term.

Genes And Ideas

Think about what really matters in life. All we leave behind in this world are genes and ideas. Money and wealth are transient, and riches can be sacked, just ask the Egyptians. Genes and ideas – this is the stuff of lasting legacies.

By the year 2010, the populations of many Western nations were in steep decline, while at the same time the population of China was nearing a peak of 1,400 millions. The West had been winning the ideas war in innovation, invention, literature and cultural dominance since the Renaissance. The Chinese had been winning the genes war, and to celebrate the victory, those 1.4 billion people needed living space.

There was really no place to go but north. For a nation with the capability of putting arms in the hands of 200,000,000 people, and marching them, this prospect made complete sense. For China, long a victim of the imperial excesses of the former Russian Empire, it was poetic justice to retake lost real estate from a weakened neighbor.

The time to march had arrived.

Chinese Aircraft Carriers, Particle Beams, Satellite Killers & Boomers

In June of 1982, China fired its very first submarine launched intercontinental ballistic missile, joining an elite group of five nations with such capabilities. In 1996, U.S. intelligence was somewhat surprised when the Chinese purchased an aircraft carrier from Spain, assuming only that it would be reverse engineered, trained upon, and then scrapped for steel, which the Chinese Navy promptly did.

In 2006, after successfully sending men safely into orbit for the third time in as many years, and distinguishing itself as only the third nation to have ever done so, China abruptly announced an ambitious moon landing and moon base program, alarming the Americans, who had last been to the moon three decades earlier. Then, under Washington's careful watch, the PRC began testing space-based particle beams, quickly demonstrating great success with this new class of weapons, and placing China's space weaponry on a par with that of the U.S.

Then, in 2009, to the complete amazement of the entire world, China launched an aggressive program to build five aircraft carriers, joining the United States amongst the world's premier blue water navies. The announcement heralded the arrival of China as a global Superpower, as defense analysts wisely reckoned that the only use for aircraft carriers was power projection.

Most alarming to Washington, in 2010, China declared possession of a unique class of 'several dozen suicide satellites,' evidently previously deployed, whose stated purpose was to maneuver within 10 meters of enemy satellites before violently self destructing. While the U.S. had studied such weapons, and while the shuttle had tested offensive capabilities while deployed, the U.S. found itself with nothing to match this new class of weapons, and rapidly sought the development of a matching threat.

Chinese defense analysts correctly surmised that until the West developed sufficient countermeasures, if so directed, the U.S.'s vaunted satellite controlled target acquisition, global command and control systems, military communications systems and intelligence collection capabilities could be dealt a crippling first blow, if needed.

All from a nation that as recently as 1979 had more water buffalo-dragged plows than tractors, more cat-hole outhouses than flush toilets, more bicycles than automobiles, and half a population without access to electricity.

China had arrived, leapfrogging past the technologies the U.S. had taken the latter part of the 20th Century to master, now running right alongside the dazed Americans.

Intelligence Collection Differences

The United States and the People's Republic of China go about the business of intelligence collection in entirely different ways. The U.S., with its mammoth $440 billion annual defense expenditures and $20 billion black budgets, throws incredible amounts of dollars and assets into intelligence, focusing on exploiting technology. During the Cold War, entire oceans were crisscrossed with a vast system of anti-submarine sensors, set to detect even the slightest engine noise signatures from the quietest Soviet subs. The system is still in place and working.

China, partly as an outgrowth of its huge low-wage population, in combination with an historically poor population and the government's lack of adequate defense expenditures, focuses on exploiting human intelligence (HUMINT). Very frequently, the Chinese will anoint intelligence operatives, minting agents out of willing travelers in fields as disparate as sports, entertainment, students who will be studying abroad in target countries, business exchange participants, tourist industry ombudsmen, and diplomatic corps members. These persons do an outstanding job of combing through the world's print and electronic media, gathering facts on peoples and industries for the Motherland.

Utilizing its nominal coastal defenses, China also outfits many of its fishing vessels as listening posts, outfitting its offshore islands and oil platforms with listening devices, and for deep sea, anti-submarine monitoring, dropping sonobouys from aircraft, much like the U.S. used to do back in its Vietnam War days, using P-3 Orions.

The U.S., for its part, also uses HUMINT, but prefers to utilize its vast lead in technology, focusing on the rapid deciphering of signals intelligence (SIGINT).

Here's how it works: Deep in the heart of the National Security Agency, a series of CRAY computers, performing trillions of computations per second using floating dynamic random access memory, do the task of searching for needles in a haystack of communications.

When the U.S. spy wants to focus on a particular target – she simply informs the CRAY system that she wants to study, for example, all Chinese Mandarin voice and fax communications from August 1st through December 31st, 2005, originating or received in northern China. The computer asks her to type in the keywords (or coverwords) she is looking for, and she types in "warhead", "U-238", and "kryton".

The computer then asks if she wants the rest of the traffic either before, after (or both) 15, 30, 45 or 60 seconds from when the keywords came up in conversation. Minutes later, after having scanned every single conversation sent electronically anywhere on earth (not using two cups and a string, or sunlight reflected by obsidian glass) for the engrams containing the selected Chinese words, the American spy gets a pile of traffic emailed to her, for careful analysis, with a detailed mapping software showing source, destination, avatars, and subject matter.

U.S. / P.R.C. Balance Of Trade – The Greatest Transfer Of Wealth Ever

From the reawakening of the Chinese economy in the late 1970s all the way through the first decade of the 21ˢᵗ Century, more wealth was transferred from the United States to China than had ever occurred bilaterally in history.

The trade imbalance got so bad that by the middle part of the '00s, China was running annual balance of trade surpluses of over $200 billion with the U.S. It all worked very smoothly. The massive cargo ships arrived at the great American ports in places like Long Beach, Seattle and Oakland, low to the water, heavily laden with thousands of cargo containers, with familiar names like COSCO, HANJIN, OOCL and MAERSK. Upon arrival, the ships docked, greeted by massive arms, swinging the cargo containers off the ships, back and forth, all day long, like metronomes keeping beat to the music of commerce, and the sound of the whirr of monies being transferred at light speed across the Pacific Ocean, arriving at the great Chinese banks in places like Hong Kong, Shanghai, Shenzhen and Tianjin.

Most Americans never paused to think about the scale of the economic damage being done to their country as it exported wealth at such a high rate. A two hundred billion dollars, in a year's time, amounted to $500 million per day, or $21 million per hour, or $350,000 per minute, or nearly $6,000 per second.

Visiting China, one could easily see where the monies were going, from the mahogany paneling on the walls of the gleaming new office buildings on the coasts, to the modern, efficient airports under construction all over the country, to the vastly improved infrastructures being put in place within major cities, to the brand new telecommunications gear being retrofitted where old land lines once ran, to the array of brand new, much improved munitions being purchased to upgrade the better trained Chinese armed services.

The Americans were happy to keep the deal going, securing a cheap source for their insatiable appetite for cheap imports, and the Chinese were only as happy to oblige, growing their economy, fueling the rise of the nation, and amassing huge cash reserves for reinvestment.

It was exactly what the Yanks did to the Brits between the Wars. Only this time, the center of wealth was moving much farther to the west, across the Pacific, to East Asia.

A Seduction Tale

While the U.S. had, for decades, been hemorrhaging dollars to the Chinese for their cheap imports, the Chinese had made life easy for the Americans, feeding the American cow a rich diet of reinvestment through U.S. debt purchases, keeping the American economy rolling at high speed with low interest rates.

In total, the Chinese purchases of U.S. debt slowly accumulated, until China owned, outright, over 10% of the entire U.S. national debt. This resulted in a symbiotic economic relationship, as the Chinese needed a strong U.S. economy to keep up its export growth, while the U.S. needed foreign investment in government debt to allow the continuing massive federal borrowing at low interest rates.

It was a very convenient mutual seduction, enriching China, depleting America, and fueling global economic growth. It also could not be sustained indefinitely.

Iran's Silkworm Surprise

Iran sat astride the northern bend of the Straights of Hormuz, and for years, had espoused a strategy of controlling this strategic waterway, claiming it as its own. Iran's Navy was no match for that of the United States, and never would be, so outright control of the waterway was out of the question.

Long before China became a net importer of light sweet crude oil, one of its key strategic partnerships was a special relationship with Iran, which it considered capable of disrupting the West's flow of oil. Toward these ends, for over two decades, it exported hundreds of Silkworm missiles to the Iranians.

The Silkworm was China's signature cruise missile. At 20 feet, six inches in length, with a 9'2" span, a 29.5 inch diameter and a range of 50 miles, the powerful little missile weighed 5,500 pounds, sending its 852 pound payload smashing into ships at a speed of Mach .8.

Anyone who remembers the deadly efficiency of the French-made Exocet missiles used by the Argentines against the British Navy, sinking the HMS Stark in the Falklands War of 1982 can reckon the potential threat represented by the Silkworms. The Chinese Silkworms were considered to be on a par with the French Exocets.

In a response to the rising hostilities of 2010, in a sudden and unexpected move that shocked the West, immediately raising spot oil prices to over $150 per barrel, Iran announced that it had deployed no less than 900 Silkworm missiles, ostensibly to "...protect the interests of the Islamic Republic in the face of a rapidly growing American and British naval presence in the Persian Gulf."

If warships of the British Navy could fall prey to anti-ship missiles, oil tankers were sitting ducks.

Strangely, American satellite intelligence began picking up an unusual amount of non-military Iranian shipping traffic of all kinds, oddly, moving southward toward the Iranian port city of Bandar al-Abbas.

For the first time, the price of a gallon of gas exceeded $5, as U.S. consumers drastically cut their spending, sending global markets reeling.

The Pinch Of The Umbilical Cord

The Silkworm missiles did their work with extreme efficiency. The Iranians, plunging these deadly missiles into any ship that could be floated into the Straights of Hormuz, from garbage scow to mothballed tanker, quickly sank more than a hundred ships.

The resulting damaged vessels, once scuttled, began to pile upon one another at the bottom of the shallow straight, quickly and effectively raising the ocean bottom, and making the Straight navigable only to ships with very high drafts. Mega-tankers, riding low to the waves and laden with light sweet crude oil, were out of the question. The Persian Gulf had been transformed into a trap for all but the smallest of ships.

Half the West's oil imports were no longer deliverable. The effects were devastating, and felt immediately on the spot markets, with prices tripling, and then tripling again, as panic gripped the markets. Then, slowly at first, followed with ever quickening speed, the supplies of oil worldwide began to exhaust themselves. Even the United States, with its mighty 80 day supplies safely stored in the Louisiana salt domes of its Strategic Oil Reserves, began to ration gasoline, heating oil and natural gas, as it began to run out of oil, its economy grinding to a halt.

It was going to be a hard winter in the West, and the beginnings of an economic depression were seen all over the world's great economies. Iran was to blame, and the world was furious.

The West began to plan for war against Iran, occupation of both shores of the Straight, and removal of the scuttled ships.

The Great RMB/USD Revaluation

Long berated by the Americans, who had grown increasingly tired of being beaten up economically by the Chinese, with seemingly never ending $200 billion trade imbalances as a result of the Chinese currency being artificially pegged to the value of a dollar, the Chinese finally revalued the Yuan in 2005. This 2% revaluation, more symbolic than anything, did nothing to stanch the hemorrhage of dollars from North America to East Asia. In fact, in 2005, a record $200 billion trade deficit was set between China and the United States.

Reacting to the increasingly furious Americans, who were no longer satisfied with China's continuing purchases of U.S. debt, in 2006, 2007 and 2008, the Chinese again revalued their currency in very small increments.

It did not have the desired effect, as the U.S. continued to export jobs and dollars to China, importing cheaply produced, but increasingly sophisticated and expensive goods in return. Something drastic had to be done.

Finally, China announced that it would allow the value of the Yuan to float freely against all world currencies. The results were immediate, as the world's financial markets and currency traders increasingly put faith in the currency of China, what with its huge trade surpluses, massive annual current account surpluses, tremendous cash holdings and overwhelming G-8 debt purchases.

Soon, to the surprise of few, the value of the Yuan nearly matched that of the U.S. dollar. Out of respect to this new economic reality, the OPEC cartel stopped trading light sweet crude oil in dollars, switching instead to Yuan. This acted only to increase the fall of the U.S. Dollar, raising the price of oil for Americans, offsetting the gains of increasingly affordable U.S. denominated exports with tremendously higher production costs.

In a vicious economic double-whammy, as the price of Chinese imports rose, alongside vastly more expensive energy costs, with the value of the U.S. dollar falling, a furious inflation returned to the U.S., raising interest rates, stagnating American economic growth, eating into the savings of Americans living on fixed incomes.

The results were devastating, as inflation turned into hyper-inflation, and the U.S. Federal Reserve, unable to stimulate the moribund economy through manipulation of the federal funds rate, chose instead to print even more dollars, escalating the waves of inflationary pressures, over-stimulating an economy with too many dollars chasing too few goods.

The only positive effect of the hyperinflation was the lessening of U.S. national debt, in effect making the dollars worth dimes, and the dimes worth pennies. Those who had jobs realized tremendous income gains as wages rose as rapidly as prices. Those on fixed incomes, especially the elderly, saw savings wiped out, and desperately tried to get by in the new age of hyperinflation.

Globally, with its massive national debt and hyperinflation, the U.S. was increasingly seen as the world's greatest 'banana republic', an economic basket case. The Chinese manufacturing sector suffered with shrinking exports, but the economy more than made up for the export losses by snapping up on dollar denominated assets, purchasing U.S. land and companies at bargain sale prices.

And so the Americans had finally gotten their wish, after decades of 8 Yuan to the dollar, with huge governmental borrowing alongside massive trade deficits, the exchange rate finally settled at two U.S. Dollars per one Chinese Yuan. A new economic powerhouse had arrived, as Chinese denominated foreign investments surged, and China flexed her new found muscle.

The Great Betrayal

The United States had long touted its treasury bonds as the world's safest investment, and they were – guaranteed by the U.S. government itself.

But by the time the U.S. Dollar had crashed to a value of less than half a Chinese Yuan, the Chinese simply stopped purchasing U.S. debt.

Put off at first, in response, the U.S. raised interest rates to increase foreign purchases of U.S. debt. When this didn't work, desperate for the continuing infusions of cash that allowed the U.S. government to borrow, a surprising result occurred, as U.S. politicians began to express the desire to get their fiscal house in order.

The result was a war of sorts between the two U.S. political parties, with partial governmental shutdowns, long delays in budget approvals, drastic cuts in spending, and large increases in taxation.

Since debt could no longer be issued, and with the American government no longer able to borrow to finance its overspending, the budget finally came under the mighty axe. Desperate times required desperate measures, and to the surprise of all, the first area to be cut was servicing the national debt, which had grown into the fifth largest national budget item.

The U.S. announced a one year moratorium on reimbursements of any debt holdings, in effect, reneging on its national debt.

Confidence in the United States sank, the dollar tanked further, and the world, long accustomed to giving back to the U.S. by financing its national government's largesse, was betrayed.

Of course, those nations with large U.S. debt holdings, China being the predominant holder of U.S. debt, were infuriated.

A Very Unusual Defection Story

Probe your enemy's defenses – test his tolerances, and find his weaknesses, so wrote the great Chinese defense mind Sun Tzu, in his landmark work studied for centuries in military academies worldwide – *The Art of War.*

The lasting geopolitical lessons learned from good intelligence never lose their value. The dates and times of these events remain deliberately vague, but the timeframe could be late in the year 2009, as Japan rapidly rearms, and dangerous tensions exist between an increasingly isolated Russian regime, a rapidly rising China, a declining America, and The Koreas – The Trigger.

* * *

At 0620 A.M., an American U-2 Black Cat thunders from an airfield 40 kilometers south of Seoul, 75 kilometers south of the Korean DMZ, the most heavily fortified border on earth. Inside the van on the hill with the little satellite dish and antennae on top, coffee cups and ashtrays shake as the jet-black U-2 gains altitude. The van is super-cooled, out of respect for its tall racks of machinery, and to the detriment of its occupants, a tightly squeezed row of smart young men and bright young women who have been trained by the United States taxpayers to listen and think in languages other than their own.

Today, the van happens to have 3 Chinese, 8 Korean, and 2 Russian Voice Processing Specialists. If youd've have asked them if they liked spying, each SigInt Op, to a person, would've scratched their heads, scanning around the van for any signs of a spy. To these professionals, this was just another routine day of collections. They were pros. Data collectors. Intel analysts. Intelligence Operatives. The best.

"Yao dong wu, yao dong wu, qing huida."

{105, 105, please answer.}

A 7.5 inch reel-to-reel tape began rolling on position 9, down on the Chinese side of the van. It was occupied by a Cat-II Op, still green, but showing lots of promise.

"Yao dong wu huida, qiluojia fang hao, qingqiu jiangluo."

{105 answering. Landing gear set, request landing.}

"DF him," the GMS told the Op.

"Yao dong wu, keyi jiangluo."

{105, permission to land granted.}

The voice was booming from China. It could've been next door.

"Yao dong wu, qifei."

{105 taking off.}

At exactly the moment of that transmission, an electronic signal left both the nose and the tail of the U-2. The signals crossed right over the easternmost tip of the Shandong Peninsula. "Its Wendeng in TOLs," said the Cat-II to the GMS.

"Yao dong wu, keyi qifei."

{105, takeoff permitted}

"Roll it, keep scanning," replied the GMS. Routine traffic – time to light another smoke.

Indeed, it started off as a very normal day of takeoffs and landings at Wendeng Airbase, located in The People's Republic of China's Shandong Province. Shandong sticks out like a sword, poking into the East China Sea, just a couple hundred miles of open water from South Korea, and a few hundred miles more from the west coast of Japan. A flight of old Mig-19's (as best as could be guessed by the sound of the throat microphones) was doing routine take-offs and landings on a smoggy, steamy August morning.

To the SigInt Ops on the ground, it was just more tedious work. The routine never changed. Load up a U-2 with receivers, cameras and other interesting electronic devices, establish a downlink, and fly the bird in an East-Asian orbit over the northernmost extent of the South Korean landmass, east toward the northern Straights of Tsushima, then back west toward the East China Sea, all day long. The traffic was always the same: old Migs doing TOLs. Occasionally, you'd get some air-to-air combat practice or air-to-ground target practice, or the stray navigation flight, or possibly a VIP transfer...but it was all routine. China was just getting off her back, her air force was far less effective than that of Israel, and a great nation was just beginning to arm herself in preparation for the 21st Century, The Chinese Century.

"Yao dong wu, zuo juan."

{105 left turning.}

"Yao dong wu, keyi zuo juan."

{105 permitted to left turn.}

In an icy, dark, air-conditioned van on the Korean peninsula, the little group of Americans linguists sat with headphones on, in front of 9 foot tall stacks of equipment, with 7.5 inch per second reel-to-reel tape recorders. 80,000 feet above, a lone U-2 pilot turned on his auto-nav and flew big, bow-tie shaped figure 8's so far up in the sky, that he had to wear a spacesuit. These Black Cat pilots were nuts. After missions, some of the SigInt Ops would head down to the ville to use their language skills on some of the locals. Some of the nice young girls found it charming indeed, to be propositioned or bought a drink by nice young Americans trained in the dialect of Korean spoken in the North, or in Chinese, or in Russian, or, as was the case with the older Ops, who still remembered Vietnamese, or other languages they might have picked up while poking their noses into books along 17 mile drive in Monterey. Not the Black Cats, though. They just liked to decompress from all that altitude.

"Yao dong er, Yao dong san, Yao dong si, keyi qifei."

{102, 103, 104, permission to take-off.}

You usually couldn't pick up the pilots until they were airborne, but this was Wendeng, and the listening conditions were perfect.

"Yao dong er, qifei."

{102 taking off.}

"Yao dong san, qifei."

{103 taking off.}

"Yao dong si, qifei."

{104 taking off.}

Sometimes after de-briefing the missions, the Black Cats would join the SigInt Ops down in the ville or down in the lounge for some beverages. These guys were all about endurance, and the Ops were all ears. "So what the hell do you do in a space suit all day, flying figure 8's at 80,000 for 8 hours?" we'd tease them. "Pee down our legs, think about drinking, and pity all you poor shivering bastards," they'd answer.

Good enough for this G.I.

At the end of the row of racks, Op 9 had a lit cigarette, a steaming cup of coffee (his fourth, it was already 6:50), and a bad hangover. But his reels were rolling, at least.

"I've still got Wendeng in TOLs...4 Mig-19s." said the intercept operator.

"Roll it, keep scanning..." came the reply from the Ground Mission Supervisor.

With two frequencies in each ear, the Sigint Op kept the receivers on the U-2 busy. It was a quiet day. These TOLs were brutal in their monotony.

"Yao dong wu, you zhuan."

{105 right turning.}

"Yao dong wu keyi you zhuan."

{105 permitted to right turn.}

It would be the last time I heard the voice of 105 until I met him the following day.

On board one of the Mig-19s, Dawei, a young pilot who later took the name 'David' left the square box formation of his comrades, diving over into a large cumulus cloud to the east, over the East China Sea. The ground controller, reading his People's Daily while sipping tea and enjoying a smoke, was as oblivious to Dawei's odd maneuver as were his fellow pilots. TOLs were the realm of young, green, sweaty-palmed pilots. The People's Liberation Air Force didn't have a lot of money to spend on fuel, so when these Mig jockeys had their brief chances to fly, it was a special day, and simply concentrating on no fuck-ups was the rule.

"Yao dong er, you zhuan."

{102, right turning.}

"Yao dong er, keyi you zhuan."

{102, right turn permitted.}

"Yao dong san, you zhuan."

{103, right turning.}

"Yao dong san, keyi you zhuan."

{103, right turn permitted.}

"Yao dong si, you zhuan."

{104, right turning.}

"Yao dong si, keyi you zhuan."

{104, right turn permitted.}

At this moment, South Korea began going to work, as had the Japanese, one hour ahead to the east. One hour behind Korea, westward toward China, it was still daybreak, and the rising sun shone brightly through the haze and puffy clouds to the east. The U-2 flew above it all, so high that he could see stars above his canopy. Far below, descending to just 50 meters above the surface of the Pacific Ocean, already riding low on fuel, a lone Mig-19 flew eastward.

"Yao dong wu, qing huida."

{105, please answer.}

105's pilot switched off his microphone, keeping his helmet on, fighting the glare. He knew he would not be returning home, never again seeing his family, never again to climb the ladder of a promising career, never again to know the sweet comforts or soft whispers of his young wife.

"Yao dong wu, qing huida."

He switched off the Mig's Identify Friend or Foe apparatus. IFF wouldn't be needed over Seoul.

"Yao dong wu, qing huida."

"Eastward. Conserve fuel. Maintain altitude. Stay on target..." Dawei focused his thoughts away from family and friends, tuning in his homing beacon to an A.M. radio station in Seoul. He understood a few of the Korean words. After all, Korean, like Japanese, Vietnamese or any other of East Asia's many languages, all borrowed heavily from Chinese, the mother tongue.

"Yao dong wu, qing huida!" Now the Ground Controller's voice was booming, which did not go by unnoticed in the van.

"Nine, clear your frequencies and stay on Wendeng."

"Roger GMS, freqs cleared." It was a strange relief to have just one frequency in both ears. Kind of like listening to an FM radio, thought Nine.

"Yao dong wu, yao dong wu, qing huida!"

"10, start scanning Qingdao and Jinan," said the GMS, snuffing out his smoke, yanking over the slack on his headphone cord, no longer pacing the van, one hand on each earphone, now.

"10, roger. Got 'em loaded, no activity on all freqs."

"Yao dong wu, yao dong wu, mashang baodao!"

{105, 105, immediately report!}

"GMS, I think we've got a splash," said Nine.

"Dittoes, Nine. That's an E-gram. Ten, keep your ears perked," said the GMS.

The message flew off to The Agency at the speed of light. "....2320 zulu, PLA Mig-19 crash, last known activity TOLS, point of origin, Wendeng Airbase."

"Yao dong wu, yao dong wu, yao dong wu, qing huida!"

Nine noticed the changing voice of the Wendeng Ground Controller. He was becoming emotional. The GMS could've sworn the Chinese GRC was weeping now.

"Yao dong wu, yao dong wu, yao dong wu, qing huida!"

"Wouldn't wanna be that poor sumbitch when he gets off work," said Ten.

"I wouldn't wanna be that Mig Jockey," said Nine.

"Stay on the freqs, girls," admonished the GMS.

At that exact moment, throughout South Korea, air raid sirens began steadily droning. But strangely, it wasn't Thursday at 10:00 A.M. In Seoul, a city of 10,000,000, taxis stopped driving, buses disgorged passengers, and people began scrambling for subway shelters. If you ask any Korean above the age of 40, they'll distinctly remember exactly where they were the morning the sirens went off. It happened the same week the 1988 Olympic Games were awarded to Seoul. It was the start of World War III. Even stoic Koreans remember this moment in time, like Americans thinking back to their Missile Crisis.

"YAO DONG WU, QING HUIDA."

A new voice now boomed through the headphones of the SigInt Ops. This one sounded like he meant business.

"GMS, Nine. I've got a simulcast in Shandong."

"GMS, Ten. I've got a simulcast in Liaoning and Shenyang."

The GMS switched his feed to both Ops.

"YAO DONG WU, QING HUIDA."

"Nine, Ten, roll 'em all," said the GMS. "Floor, I need more Chinese Ops!" Throughout the listening post his voice boomed. People, began running toward the van, when over the intercom, somebody yelled, "HTACC informs us ROKAFs have announced a Threatcon One."

"That's it", thought everyone on the Floor, and all the SigInt Ops (now doffing their headphones, hearing the drone of the air raid sirens for the first time) and all the people of the Republic Of Korea. "This is how World War III begins."

Nine kept his headphones on. The GMS yelled.

"Everyone out of the van, get down to the shelters." The van cleared.

Nine, lighting a cigarette, took a drag, staring up at the spinning reels on his rack.

"YAO DONG WU, YAO DONG WU, QING HUIDA."

Then, Nine had an idea. If wrong, he'd be sure to lose a couple of stripes. "What the hell does that matter, it's WW-III?!" He laughed at the thought. "Screw it."

He sent the Flash to The Agency. "Mig-19 Splash Doubtful - Suspect Defection."

* * *

Pyongyang wondered what in the devil the Yankee Imperialists and their lackeys in The South were up to.

Tokyo held her breath, waiting for the booms from the west, as the first blasts shook Seoul.

Moscow and Beijing were still rubbing the sleep from their eyes.

Back in Washington, an NSC operative walked a paper over to the Advisor's desk. "Get me the President."

Two minutes later, the order came back from D.C. "Advise ROK stand down, maintain ThreatCon Two."

Back in Korea, the drone of sirens finally stopped. People slowly emerged, wondering, had it been a drill all along? More saber rattling from President Chun?

* * *

As it turns out, Dawei and his Mig-19 had been circling Seoul for 5 minutes, riding on fumes, desperately tipping his wings in the pilot's international language of "Come and get me, you morons!" He was finally escorted to an airbase just north of Seoul, by several highly agitated Republic Of Korea F-4 Phantoms.

The USAF and ROKAF air defenses had missed him entirely, until the bogey had finally climbed up from his 50-meter altitude over Seoul, to avoid slamming into some of The Hub Of East Asia's taller landmarks.

The Chinese had missed him, too. Later analysis of the tapes would yield countless conversations between 102, 103 and 104. "Did you see him?" "He disappeared into a cloud." "He descended rapidly." "I never saw him." And on they went.

The next day, two ROKAF four star generals approached the flight commander's desk at HTACC. They were somber. Smartly saluting a shocked American Captain and his Korean counterpart sitting at their desks, each general, hands trembling, yanked the rows of stars from their shoulder boards, placing them on the desk.

Standing, the desk officers stood to return the salutes. The ex-generals then replied with quick bows, walking out into the morning calm under the silent stares and open admiration of their former charges. Here was honor. Here was responsibility.

The spin immediately commenced. Newspapers variously ran the headlines: "Chinese Pilot Defects." "Seoul Shudders As

Chinese Mig Slips Under Homeland Defenses." "Seoul Passes Routine Air Defense Exercise." "He Could Have Had A Nuke." "Whose Mistake?" "Back From The Brink." And on it went.

* * *

Up at the little South Korean airbase where the Mig-19 had finally landed, nearer to the Demilitarized Zone, agents from all cells of J-2 / Intelligence Division methodically combed over the vintage Mig-19. KCIA, CIA, DIA, ROKAF, USAF, J-2 operatives, every spook imaginable inspected the craft, from pitot tube to airbrakes, cockpit canopy to afterburners. It was determined that the pilot must have bought off his fuelman; no Mig in the Chinese Air Force doing TOLs would ever get enough gas to fly across the East China Sea to Korea!

Far better secrets than these gushed from the fresh translations of Dawei's flight operations manual, in a little 3-ring binder. The entire Air Order of Battle of Northeast China had been compromised. It was a treasure trove. A song was soon coined by the translators, and is still being sung in the hallways of the Defense Language Institute:

"Dawei, dawei, feijide jiashi yuan...."

{David, David, pilot of the airplane....}

"Dawei, dawei, dao da le Han Guo yuan...."

{David, David, arriving late in Korea....}

But the best Intel by far was coming from David, down in the tank, where the mood was less than jovial.

An American general and his stern Korean counterpart sat on one side of a short metal desk, while an exhausted Dawei sat on the opposite end, sipping Coca-Colas and waxing eloquent.

"Ask him how many Mig-19s there are at Wendeng."

"Ask him if he's tested any new firing mechanisms."

"Ask him if they keep any nukes at Wendeng."

"Ask him what the order of command is for using the nukes."

"Ask him what use the big green glass (in the cockpit) has."

"Ask him how long pilots have to train to fly wingman only ops."

"Ask him where he went to school."

Finally, the General tapped the translator on the arm, establishing eye-lock.

"Ask him why he defected for Freedom."

Showtime in the battle of ideologies ideologies, thought the translator.

The Generals' eyes narrowed, nodding toward the Chinese. "Ask him, airman."

But Dawei held one last surprise for his new handlers.

"Ni weishenme touben ziyou le…?" came the translated question.

{Why did you defect for Freedom?}

"Wo bushi touben ziyoule…." Dawei shifted in his seat, staring into the eyes of his handlers, pausing now, gazing at the translator, who turned back to the Generals.

"Jack him up, airman!" snapped the American General, his Korean counterpart a bit confused, now. "Get his response. Now!"

"Ni weishenma touben ziyou le…?" came the repeated question.

"Wo bushi touben ziyoule," replied a smiling Dawei. "Wo dao Hanguo lai de yuanyin shi yinwei wo yao dedao Taiwande jiubai qian kuai meijin de jin."

{I didn't defect for Freedom. The reason I came to Korea is because I want to acquire Taiwan's $900,000 in gold.}

The translator turned to the Generals, a wry smile on his face. "Sirs, with all due respect, I don't think we've got a political issue here. This guy's a businessman."

The General paused. The Korean General whispered something into the American General's ear.

"Strike that, airman."

* * *

In Beijing, the career Party official smiled across his raised glass of tea, gazing at the military man with a new respect.

"It worked, didn't it?" asked the Vice Premier.

"Tremendously, sir," replied the Air Forces Marshall, beaming. "Their defenses always assumed too much."

"So much is proven."

"Every Korean is extremely nervous. Trust in the Americans is almost non-existent."

The Vice Premier, picking up a cell phone, then commanded an unknown recipient in very cryptic words.

"Launch the reunification."

"Ming Bai!" came the immediate reply.

The North Korean Putsch & Korean Reunification

For the longest time, most acutely in fact, since the end of World War Two and the Communist Revolution of 1949, China's aim had been to reassert herself as the regional power, returning East Asia to the balance it had enjoyed for over two millennia. Unfortunately, although the Japanese had replaced the jigsaw puzzle of territorialities and influences left by centuries of meddling by the colonial powers, the Japanese defeat left a vacuum that had been rapidly filled by the Americans.

But even the American grip on the region had been slowly weakening, with the losses of bases in Thailand, Taiwan, Vietnam, the Philippines, and most of the Ryukyu Islands. Japan was out of the question – she had always been too strong to dominate, and as an island, was separate from the Asian mainland. The only toehold remaining for American forces in the Chinese theater was the Korean Peninsula. In the early 1950s, China had attempted to eject the Yankee presence there, only to receive a million death bloody nose from the better equipped Americans.

The lesson had been learned, and the only logical way to get rid of the Americans once and for all was to let the Koreans take care of matters themselves. The North could never destabilize the South as long as the Americans were there, China had long realized the lost cause in such a Cold War pipe dream. The charade that had started with a just leadership in Kim Il-Song, had slowly degenerated, madly careening into unstable rule of the pedophile and drunkard Kim Jong-Il, who was preparing his own son's succession and building a nuclear arsenal. Kim's idiocy ran unabated, while continuing poor harvests required great amounts of Chinese assistance.

The only way to make the Koreans comfortable enough to let their American allies depart was to allow reunification. The time had arrived. The operation would be remarkably simple in its execution.

Kim Jong-Il was summoned to the Chinese Ambassador's residence just minutes before midnight.

The Chinese attaché did not mince words. "Mr. Kim, by order of the governing council of the Chinese People's Republic, your time as leader here has ended. Please come with me." Without a word, the Dear Leader followed the attaché through a back door, down a long hallway, up three flights of stairs, and into a waiting MI-8 helicopter.

Upon Kim's arrival in Dandong, he was escorted to a waiting limousine, driven three kilometers out of town, pushed out of the auto, and shot once in the back of the head. Placing the corpse on top of a blue-sheeted stretcher, frontal photographs of the dead leader were taken. One of the assassins asked the group, widely grinning, "Should we send his family a bill for the bullet?!" Laughter broke out, as the body was pulled, then rolled, then kicked into a shallow grave.

The next day, the North Korean Cabinet Ministers were fully briefed on Mr. Kim's sudden illness, and very poor prognosis for recovery. "We would be very surprised if Mr. Kim survives the night," declared a Chinese informant, passing pictures of a very dead Kim around the table, as the reality of the situation slowly sank in amongst the ministers. "In the interim, we will be increasing our aid, moving our advisors into your border regions for increased exchanges with the South, and providing you with key day to day operational directives. Is this understood?"

The ministers nodded, their smiles slowly disappearing. There was a new boss in town, invisible and powerful, and oddly, acting in much the same way as did the old boss.

To the South Korean President's office came a terse message from Beijing. "The end of the despicable regime in the north is come. We will support the reunification of the great Korean peoples in all respects, both diplomatically and economically, under one condition: all American forces must depart.

It was an offer the South could not refuse, and after brief debate, a carefully timed series of events were agreed upon, starting with a complete opening of the border, food and medicine exchanges, northern demobilization, elections, and then on to full unification. Based upon the German model, the Chinese knew that with the shape the north had been in, the simple process of reunifying would occupy Korea for decades.

It would be a nice project for them, a reunified Korea would offer new competition for the hated Japanese, and finally, the Americans would be asked to leave.

Nuclear Korea!

For over a thousand years, the Korean people had demonstrated a proclivity for going it alone, showing respect for their neighbors, but preferring to live and act on their own. For this reason, the great King Sejong had invented the unique and logical Korean alphabet, allowing for confidentiality in communications amongst Koreans, and greater independence from their powerful Japanese and Chinese neighbors. For these reasons (and many more), Korea had earned a reputation as something of a turtle, even proudly building an armada of ironclad naval vessels in the shape of turtles, defeating the Japanese and keeping the peninsula independent.

Fiercely Buddhist and largely Confucian in values, the Koreans had come to be known amongst respectful East Asians as "The Hermit Kingdom," and for very good reason. When dealing with Korea, it was best to expect the unexpected, treat all sides with respect, and not allow appearances to deceive.

The newly unified Korea immediately set about the great task of stitching together what nearly four generations of separation had kept apart. Tearful family reunions were held, babies were fed, whole villages were introduced to modern agricultural techniques, the natural resources of the north were soon tapped, tourism rose, and the media made it play out like a grand soap opera.

The Americans had been surprisingly obliging in accepting the offer of departure which they really could not refuse, having been long occupied in the Global War On Terror, forces stretched thin. To thank the United States, the Koreans very graciously offered a week long celebration touted as "The Victory Of Liberty," flying any and all interested American veterans who had served in Korea, and their families, to a series of banquets, parades, dances, tours, and receptions. It was a fitting end to a tremendous investment of time, effort and resources by the American people, and even though Washington could sense another great power shift taking place, the images being broadcast were so intoxicating and reaffirming, no one paused to suspicion hidden hands at work. To the Americans, it just seemed as if Liberty had won yet another battle over tyranny. Only the American military experts were disturbed, not only at losing a base of operations so close to a growing Chinese threat, but also at the prospect of their Korean friends operating independently of their giant neighbors to the west.

This point was not lost on the Koreans, and a very Korean decision was made, announced to a surprised world in the most mundane of terms.

"The Korean people, to assure the continued peace, independence and prosperity of greater East-Asia, will maintain a defensive nuclear arsenal of no fewer than 1,000 warheads. The former weapons of the north will be dismantled, and those that existed in the south will be augmented."

And so, in but an historical eye-blink, the world now had, in its 11th largest economy, its fourth strongest nuclear power.

The Chinese, astonished, quietly protested via diplomatic channels, knowing that any future meddling would be severely limited by the presence of these weapons. Korea was to be a player, and would best be left alone.

The Great Japanese Awakening

Anyone familiar with the history of Japan, from the time of the Shoguns and through bushido culture, and then through the great Meiji Restoration and the military innovations of the 20th Century, knows that it was only through the imposition of a peace constitution by the United after the Second World War, that the nation's defenses were largely ignored.

In fact, Article 9 of the Japanese Constitution expressly forbade the development of any military forces that were non-defensive in nature. This, in combination with the ruinous aftermaths of the atomic bombings in Hiroshima and Nagasaki, as well as the fire bombings of Tokyo and other major cities, had produced a very powerful Japanese peace lobby.

The American nuclear umbrella, as well the basing of the American 7th fleet, as well as the huge military outlays of the 'older brother' Americans, had long allowed Japan, the world's second largest economy, to get by on the cheap defensively. But now, with the American withdrawal from Korea, an American military increasingly distracted by the fight against terrorism, the rising Chinese threat, and now, nuclear Korea, the time to reassert power and influence had arrived. Domestically, this was not a hard sell, especially to a Japanese public still stinging from the rejection of the Chinese not allowing Japan to join the United Nations Security Council as a permanent member.

To the Japanese, long accustomed to financing huge national projects featuring the expenditure of trillions of yen on massive engineering feats, rearming would come easy. The Chinese blue water navy would be matched, aircraft carrier for aircraft carrier. The self-defense forces would be augmented to a level of one million soldiers, with mandatory national service. The development of highly sophisticated air defenses, including an impenetrable missile shield, would be accomplished, alongside an equally airtight submarine and naval defense perimeter. In but three years, Japan's military quickly matched that of China, reestablishing Japan as a regional superpower.

On the issue of nuclear forces, the constitution would be permanently adjusted, and the establishment of a ground, seaborne, airborne, and yes, a spaceborne nuclear deterrent, twice as large as Korea's, would be established.

For Japan, a longtime producer and consumer of nuclear power, finding enough fissile material was no problem, nor was achievement of the technological prowess to construct powerful, accurate warheads. In short order, Japan possessed over 2,000 nuclear devices, and the militarization of space was soon matched by the Chinese, Russians and Americans.

From the Kuriles down through the Ryukyus, it was to be Fortress Japan, once again. In ousting American Influence from East-Asia, the Chinese soon realized that it had unexpectedly reawakened a powerfully remilitarized Japan.

Keeping the hated Japanese at bay would occupy much effort, great expenditures of wealth, and much strategic planning.

Light Sweet Crude And Sea Lanes

The life-blood of the world economy was oil. Sea shipping lanes were the life giving arteries of this life blood. The world had three major arteries: Hormuz, Panama, and Malucca. Shut these down, and the world economy's heart stops beating.

Once their Iranian allies had sealed off the Straights of Hormuz, the rest of the job was quite simple for China.

One focal point was the Panama Canal, which the U.S. had returned to the Panamanians late in the 20th Century, and in which China had heavily invested, from 1990 onwards. For the Chinese, it was simply a matter of moving the weapons of choice into place – the maps were all very fresh.

The other focal point was the Straits of Malucca, geographically very near the Chinese mainland, separating Indonesia from Malaysia. It didn't take any kind of powerful, blue water navy to get the job done – just lots of mines, a few submarine launched cruise missiles, and a handful of anti-ship missiles.

In a lightning attack, just three days after the Iranian surprise, with energy markets already reeling and global stock markets in a full retreat, the Chinese attacked. When they were finished, the sunken hulks of dozens of ships, many of them ironically loaded with Chinese cargo, lay strewn about the shallow depths of these two strategic waterways, blocking all traffic, military, civilian or otherwise.

Most galling, the hulk of the aircraft carrier USS Theodore Roosevelt, stricken by dozens of missiles and listing at 30 degrees, lay dead in the waters of the Panama Canal.

The global economy, suffering a major heart attack, began grinding to a near halt, save for air travel. It would be months before the sea lanes could be reopened, if then.

In an act of ostensible friendship, China offered immediate assistance to their allies in Iran, sending 'stabilizing troops.' To the Panamanians and Indonesians came kind offers of immediate rebuilding and security, in exchange for military bases, of course. It was a naked power play, being orchestrated in ways that left no doubts in the minds of Western analysts.

Evidently, by hook or by crook, the 21st Century was going to be very Chinese.

The Sordid Tale Of Hughes, Loral, Motorola & Clinton

During the run-up to the election of 1996, pitting, in Bill Clinton, an embattled incumbent young President who had most recently lost the Congress to a rebellious class of '94 House Republicans, against an aging Bob Dole, lion of the Party and flag bearer of the Republican Cause, things were desperate for the Democrats. Ultimately, it was all about raising campaign dollars and appealing to white women, which the President needed to do in order to win in the suburbs.

On the border between Highland Park and Lincolnshire, Illinois, up in the northern suburbs of Chicago where the Cub fans proudly dwell, the battle lines were drawn, and there was money to be made. In a tony neighborhood right off of highway 22 not far from Michael Jordan's place, there was going to be a quick two hour fundraiser at one of the mansions, the President was coming, and there were millions to be scored.

Sometime before the party, a call was placed to the White House by one Mr. Galvin, the CEO of Schaumburg, Illinois based Motorola Corporation, a communications giant, also located in the northern suburbs of Chicago. Galvin had a favor to ask for, as Motorola had invested over a billion dollars in its Project Iridium, a global system of geosynchronous orbiting satellites that would allow for a mega-boom in wireless telecommunications. It appeared that with the slow paced recovery of the Space Shuttle fleet after yet another grounding, launches were coming too slowly, and it would take more desperate means to successfully complete its Project Iridium.

Galvin asked the President if there was any way he could find alternative launch vehicles for the precious Iridium communications satellites.

"Alternatives?" queried the President.

"Yes, perhaps some of our older Atlas Centaurs, or our friends at the ESA, hell, I don't care if you put the birds on old

Titans, just as long as they can be deployed safely," implored Galvin.

"Aren't those satellites technologically sensitive?"

"You bet they are. They've got the very best we have."

"What about the Chinese? Their Long March deliveries are cheap, and getting fairly reliable..." the President trailed off.

"Sir," replied Galvin, "there are technologies at play here that I'm certain are protected from export to the Chinese communists. Not to mention, their Long March missiles aren't very reliable."

Galvin was right. As recently as February 15, 1996, less than 30 seconds after a Chinese Long March rocket was fired from a launch pad in southern China, the booster malfunctioned, exploding, along with a $200 million American satellite, owned by a team of scientists from Hughes Electronics Corporation and Loral Space & Telecommunications Ltd., who launched a detailed accident investigation. The Chinese had lost face, and a detailed analysis of the many problems associated with the Chinese booster included a plethora of suggestions on how to avoid future repeats of the mishap. The main problem had to do with flight guidance system glitches.

"You let me worry about most favored nation trading status, and let me see what I can do about the Chinese," said Clinton.

Clinton had already taken care of COCOM, the Coordinating Committee for Multilateral Export Controls, a group of concerned Western nations that had successfully limited weapons technology transfers to the Soviet Bloc and China. It was among the first to go in the 1993 round of export control reforms, even with promises to replace it with the 1996 Wassenaar Arrangement on Export Controls for Conventional Arms and Dual Use Goods and Technologies.

"Say, by the way, I'm gonna be up in Chicago in a few days – can we count on you?" he added.

Galvin knew a fundraising pitch when he heard one, and he also knew he had been checkmated. "Thank you for your support, Mr. President. You can count on us."

* * *

The President discreetly tasked an aide to find a way to ask the Chinese what it would take to get the Motorola birds up in the air fast, via their nascent satellite launch and delivery service, entirely State-run.

In March of 1996, the Clinton Administration silently shifted authority over licensing satellites from the State Department to the Commerce, doing an end around on the Senate Foreign Relations Committee, which would no longer need to be informed.

It ended up happening in a strange way. A Chinese government contact was identified, through a Chinese-American fundraiser of all people, and the price was set at roughly $35 - 80 million per launch. Problem was, there were strings attached, as the Chinese seemed very intent on securing some vital technologies to help advance their launch delivery systems.

The Chinese really needed to know what the Americans had mastered in the key areas of staging, and timing devices. The staging technologies also had serious applications when it came to making intercontinental ballistic missiles run on time and accurately. The timing devices also had applications in producing the maximum explosive yield from low-yield nuclear devices. But how to transfer these technologies?

To keep away from the careful watch of U.S. government oversight authorities, proxy technology transfers were established, through Hughes Corporation, and then through a little known aerospace firm called Loral, with excellent Malaysian and Chinese connections. The transfers were made, the launches went off impeccably, and the Chinese became excellent partners. Everyone was happy, especially the Chinese, who leap-frogged into real players in the ICBM business, and effective warhead deliveries for their 400 nuclear devices.

As it turned out, all the fiber optic cable that had been lain down during the 1990s run-up to the Great Tech Crash following Y2K had created a bandwidth glut, and Mororola's Project Iridium was a miserable failure.

The technology transfers to the Chinese government, especially in the key areas of staging and timing devices, saved the Chinese an estimated 20 years of development costing over 30 billion dollars. The Pentagon admitted that the technology that so vastly improved the Long March missile also rendered China's Dong Feng strategic nuclear missile series, almost identical to the Long March missiles, much more deadly.

According to Dana Rohrbacher, (R., California), Chairman of the House Space and Aeronautics subcommittee, in a House speech on April 30, 1996, U.S. expertise had "perfected" China's Long March rockets. "Engineers from Loral, assisted by engineers from Hughes electronics, and at the direction of their superiors, charged forward to correct the problems in the Long March. It seems that what happened was a sterile, coldly calculated decision to fix these problems with no consideration of the national security implications to the United States."

He added, "Chinese missiles blowing up on launch is a good thing. We should not be making their missiles better."

Bill Gertz, Defense and National Security correspondent for the Washington Post, reported to Representative Rohrbacher, saying that an aerospace engineer from Motorola was telling him that the company was involved in upgrading Chinese space boosters / missiles under a national security waiver signed by the President. According to Rohrbacher, Motorola supplied rocket stage separation technology, and Motorola helped the Chinese learn how to dispense satellites into orbit – MIRVing technology.

Thus did the United States give away, in the 1990s, more than men died to protect, at Los Alamos, in the 1940s.

Chinese ICBMs – Mini-Warheads & Electromagnetic Pulse Warfare

Matching the newly acquired technologies with an already well developed space program and advanced military techniques, the Chinese very quickly established an entirely new set of intercontinental ballistic missiles, based upon the design of the proven Long March Three launch vehicle.

Innovating on the design and using American provided W-88 mini nuclear warhead technologies, as well as key missile staging technologies, the Chinese soon deployed hundreds of mini-warheads atop long-range missiles, publicly announcing a three-pronged strategy of national defense in the event of attack:

1. Retaliation against enemy population centers, to disable the people.
2. Destruction of all enemy satellites, space based weapons, and any other orbiting assets, to disable the military command, control and communications.
3. Offensive use of electromagnetic pulse devices, particularly over enemy urban and technological centers, to disable the economy.

To worried defense analysts in Washington, the Chinese strategy sounded more offensive than defensive. Worse yet, the Chinese knew that the United States could not adequately defend against the strategy, and it was a return to the timeworn Cold War standoff of mutually assured destruction.

Most worrisome perhaps was the fact that the Americans had much more to lose than the Chinese.

Repatriating Taiwan

After the 2008 Olympics were over, international pressure on the Chinese to 'be good' in relations with Taiwan effectively ceased. The government in Taiwan had done everything but declare its independence, and, particularly galling to the Communists in Beijing, continued making major arms purchases from the Americans.

The pressure on Taiwan started with the daily over flights of missiles of all types from China, over the narrow Straights of Taiwan, and over Taiwan proper. To add to the nervousness of the protesting Taiwanese, China began amassing a 200,000 man military force in nearby Fujian province, with over 100 naval vessels, ostensibly for defensive maneuvers, but not coincidentally geared for a major amphibious assault.

After similar jockeying in 1996, the United States had loudly moved 2 aircraft carrier battle groups into the South China Sea, one of these within the Taiwan Straits itself. But that was back in the days when China did not own over one-tenth of the United States' national debt outright, when the Chinese military was considerably weaker, and when China's economy had barely joined the top ten of the world's major economic powers. This time, in spite of significant floor time given to speeches about the U.S. role in the support of Liberty worldwide, about Claire Chennault and the Flying Tigers of World War Two, and debates on Chinese expansionism, the Department of Defense, with the President's approval, decided to stand down for the time being. Wouldn't want to do anything to provoke a war, went the reasoning.

These efforts were followed by the nationalization of all Taiwanese owned or operated industries and assets, effectively stealing one fifth of Taiwan's wealth from Taipei, which caused a steep crash of the Taiwan Dollar, and angry protestations to the Taiwanese government by the major economic players, whose interests were not in the color of flags flying over office buildings or other such trivialities, but in the color of money.

Asian money markets reeled, the Taiwan bourse nearly crashed, and all the smart money began to leave Taiwan.

Then came the biggest surprise of all – a purely Chinese, publicly enunciated ultimatum. In a communiqué to the Taiwanese President, the Premier of China offered the following choice, very clearly enunciated: Acknowledge the sovereignty of China over Taiwan, fly the Red Chinese flag, assume status as a province of greater China, and relinquish all national defenses to the motherland; or – face a forced repatriation with hundreds of thousands of casualties. "The people of Taiwan will be allowed, just as is the case in Hong Kong, to keep all of their political and economic systems," added the Premier.

The Taiwanese President, desperate, announced Taiwan's possession of no fewer than 200 nuclear weapons, which he declared would be used against any invading forces, not to be limited to the field of battle. Beijing responded with silence, declining offers of diplomacy from around a world startled and frightened at the prospect of Chinese nuclear war.

In Taipei, after a tense three days of street panic, protests, and desperate, emotional debate in the parliament, and realizing no pledges of support from the United Nations, only tepid lip service from the United States, and a few pledges of mutual friendship from some African nations who had been the recipients of Taiwanese aid, Taipei gave in to Beijing's demands.

China no longer had its Cuba, and the Chinese people no longer had self-rule. In Beijing, there were street celebrations, as televised shots of Chinese fighters and bombers landing at Chang Kai Shek International Airport preceded the arrival of cadres of Chinese functionaries, led by the Foreign Minister. Financial markets began to settle down, and a world relaxed.

To those who had been around a half century beforehand, the mood in Taiwan resembled occupied Berlin after the wall went up.

The 200,000,000 Man March

With her economy in steep decline following the currency revaluations and market tumult, and increasingly isolated internationally, China's ranks of unemployed swelled to levels not seen since the 1930s. The Chinese leadership, increasingly wary of the growing street demonstrations, and worse, wholesale revolts in six large cities, feared even worse yet to come, perhaps another revolution. It was high time, they realized, to pull out an old, historically sound, time proven dissent quelling stand-by.

The search for the sorely needed external enemies didn't take long. The military, flush with the recent success in Taiwan, announced the formation of a 'Grand People's Militia' whose purpose would be to retake the initiative by marching 200 million citizens northwards, to retake the lands that belonged to Greater China, and had been stolen by the Russians two centuries ago through bad treaties. The People's Militia would also solve the growing unemployment problem, while returning much of the natural resource wealth of these northern lands. But how best to retake these lands from the Russians and Kazakhs?

After escalating the formal complaint making process in the United Nations and drum beating in the Chinese press, then taking the case to the international media and massing troops along the borders, a sight never before seen in history unfolded along the northeast and northwest Chinese borders.

Throngs of volunteers began arriving, armed mostly with handguns, or anything that could fire a bullet for that matter, dressed in the khaki and green uniforms of the militia, more often than not wearing matching green hats, although a few were lucky enough to have helmets. The pride of a nation grew as these patriots massed along the borders, awaiting the command, any command, to move northwards, retaking what belonged to China.

The first thrust was to the west, and the Kazakhs offered very little resistance. The occupying militia was overly cordial to the repatriated locals, and did an excellent job of establishing Chinese control and local administration, sweeping across the territory, right up to the border that had existed before the Treaty of Nerchinsk had been signed. The locals had never seen so many people, and as overwhelming as were the logistics of such numbers, it worked amazingly well, fueling Chinese pride.

The Russians were not as easily intimidated, and although very nervous about the massive armies forming just to the south of the Amur river in China's Heilongjiang Province, they were prepared to hold their own in fighting off a Chinese assault, even to the point, declared the Russian President, of using 'ultimate weapons.'

In a rare recollection of Sun Tzu's 'The Art Of War' admonition that the best battles never saw a single shot fired, the Chinese skillfully used a mixture of propaganda, intimidation, cajoling, carrot, and stick to pry loose the Russian grip. "Don't fire a shot," were the oft repeated orders to the militia.

Internationally, via the media, the successes of the western repatriation were shown to an increasingly acceptant world. Domestically, troops were redeployed from the northwest to the northeast borders, while the national media continued to beat the drums of war, alleging atrocious behavior by the Russians guarding the borders, insult after provocation, push after shove. Sympathies continued to flow toward the Chinese, as the U.S. volunteered to broker negotiations between the nuclear giants.

Ever prepared for the negotiation process, the Chinese came to the table with something the Russians badly needed, and that was cash wealth. The weeks of bargaining resulted in an amazing deal, a sell-off of all the lands stolen in the Treaty of Amur.

To the Russians, with a total population smaller than that of the Chinese armies massed along their southwest border, it was a face saving return to old form, with the return of this California-sized piece of real estate to the Chinese still being dwarfed by the sale of Alaska to the Americans. And the monies…what wonderful things the citizens of the largest nation on earth could do for their 170 million citizens with the 500 billion dollars in cash, and 2 trillion dollars in secured Chinese debt, and promises of peaceful coexistence from their southern neighbors.

To the Chinese, the televised images of the People's Militia retaking the northeastern lands, reassuming Greater China, were priceless. The oil, gold, and timber reserves would be fully exploited, to be certain. Getting Chinese pioneers to move northwards into the pristine lands from the crowded cities would prove easy. Even coming up with the money promised the Russians was not as much of a problem as was what to do with the millions of mobilized militia now occupying the cold lands. After all, there was a restive home population to keep occupied, and new enemies were needed.

It was high time to unite the People's Militia, turning it westward, reasoned the politburo. Another great march was organized, this one ostensibly to protect the interests of their Persian allies, who were under increasing military threat from the massing armies of the oil-starved NATO powers. The entire world watched as the great 200,000,000 Man March began, first across western China, then through the Khyber Pass, along the northern borders of Pakistan, through Afghanistan. The first Chinese began arriving in the Persian Gulf in just three weeks.

To the astonishment of their Iranian hosts, at first, the Chinese were as well fed as they were well behaved. Then, as ax met forest and the needs of 200 million 'defenders' began to manifest themselves, the Iranians could only grumble as the bargain for security turned out to be everything their land held, their people possessed, and their nation could produce for their guests.

Armageddon

When U.S. intelligence became aware of the movement out of port of all five of the Chinese aircraft carriers, they informed their Japanese allies. In one of the briefest naval battles in history, the Japanese Navy destroyed the *CNS Tang* off the coast of Dalian at 0634 GMT, and just three hours later, sunk the *CNS Hui* and *Xiong* while leaving port in Qingdao, and the *CNS Ming* and *Shang* in port, in Hong Kong.

Chinese submarines, wherever they appeared, were hunted down and destroyed by the U.S. Navy. Two factors were working in the Americans' favor, chief of which was the noisiness of the Chinese craft, and secondarily, the outstanding global system of underwater tracking devices leftover from the Cold War. In all, 26 submarines were eliminated, before the Chinese wisely decided that it would be best to leave the remainder of these assets safely out of the theater of operations.

Following these actions, the United States and Japanese navies proceeded to quarantine the Chinese coast, from the East China Sea southward through the Gulf of Tonkin, interdicting all shipping at a distance of 12 nautical miles. Chinese efforts at running the blockade were met with deck gun cannons, and the move worked extremely well.

The Chinese decided to employ the use of electromagnetic pulse warfare in disabling the Japanese-American alliance, exploding five high altitude nuclear devices over the cities of Tokyo, San Francisco, Denver, Chicago and Philadelphia. The fried chips and resultant crash of servers and backup systems resulted in the effective crash of the Internet, further disabling the global economy. In response, the Japanese exploded three high altitude nukes over the Chinese cities of Tianjin, Shanghai, and Guangdong. The effects were equally disabling.

After gathering supplies from every ship they could muster, the Chinese People's Militia moved north, joining a grand coalition calling itself The Army of Islam, which crossed the Shatt al Arab just north of Kuwait before being met by the armies of the Western powers. It was slaughter on a scale never before seen by mankind, with tens of thousands of foot soldiers firing pistols and carbines being met with tank and machine gun fire, filling the reddening waters of the Tigris and Euphrates rivers with blood. Tank treads clogged with flesh, and vehicle navigation was hindered by 40 foot piles of corpses.

Poorly supplied, hungry and thirsty wave after human wave attacked westward, only to be mowed down along a broad front roughly paralleling the riverbank. Occasionally overcoming a tank or armored personnel carrier, the armies of the East would pry open the vehicles, cutting the throats of the occupants, stealing what weapons and supplies they could.

But the wave attacks and tactics of the 18th Century were overpowered by the weapons of the 21st, and soon, the battlefields were covered by tens of millions of dead, the vast majority of whom were Chinese and Arab.

A furious Iran attacked Tel Aviv with a nuclear missile, the low-yield device destroying half the city. In retribution, utilizing devices with much higher yields, Israel struck back at the cities of Teheran and Qom, leveling them. The warning was issued – any further attacks will be met with immediate and destructive retribution.

A smallpox outbreak began in India, and quickly spread across the world. One out of five Indians died, their Pakistani and Bangledeshi neighbors faring no better, in fact, the entire Third World was most severely hit. The Western Powers, in reaction to the perceived threat from terrorists, had long earlier stockpiled vaccines sufficient to protect the majorities of their populations. When the strain of smallpox was traced directly to the Chinese, the reaction and condemnation of the world were swift. By the end of four months, the man-made epidemic had fully run its course, leaving nearly a billion dead.

The United States declared a new mutually assured destruction policy, stating that any nuclear attack on U.S. cities would result in in-kind, four-fold retaliatory attacks. Japan immediately followed with its endorsement of the policy.

Suddenly and without warning, the cities of Tokyo, London and New York were destroyed by very large nuclear devices. Western intelligence could find no source of the attacks, and no one, not even the terrorists, claimed responsibility. The nations of the world waited while the attacked looked outward, vexed, uncertain how to appropriately react.

The misery was global, with economic collapse being augmented by hunger, panic on the streets, looting, spreading disease, the breakdown of order, and finally, anarchy. Urbanized areas, those that had been considered among the lucky, having been spared the mushroom cloud, fared the worst. Migrations of survivors filled the roads, seeking respite in the countryside.

The American Hammer

"How many people have they sent to the war zone?" asked the President.

"Approximately 200,000,000," replied the Secretary of Defense.

"How many are still alive?"

"About half of them."

"They're going to have to go home sometime soon, wouldn't you think?" asked the President, cocking an eyebrow?

"That's right, sir. We already have indications of rebellions, with major movements beginning, back through Iran toward Afghanistan, and probably back across the Khyber," replied the Secretary.

"Stop them," ordered the President.

"Sir?"

"I said to stop them. Seal off their route home. Scatter them."

"But sir, we don't have the troops..." replied the Secretary.

"Then think outside the box, and pull off the gloves. I don't care how you do it, I just want those people to return home as inconvenienced as possible," said the President, adding, "I want them going home extremely pissed off."

"Very well, sir. In light of this contingency, we have a plan."

He pushed an envelope across the President's desk, caught with a hand slapping thump as it made its way to the Commander in Chief's side. The President slowly read the plan, calling for the underground detonation of two very high yield nuclear devices in the narrowest section of the Khyber Pass.

"Do it, but let the Indians, Pakistanis and Afghanis get their people out of harm's way as much as possible without giving away the plan," he instructed the Secretary.

"Very well, sir. The job will be done no later than midnight tonight."

"What about option two?"

"Mr. President, we have enough cobalt bombs to take out the top 100 Chinese urban areas. Each warhead has a 100 megaton yield."

"How many people will die?" asked the President.

"Instantly, 200 million; ultimately, 350 to 400 million," came the reply.

"Do it. Be sure to warn the Koreans and Japanese."

"God help us," said the Secretary.

"God help the Chinese," came the President's slow reply.

Indian Duplicity

If the Chinese had counted on India sitting out the war, after the numerous negotiations, parleys, side-bar conferences, and every other diplomatic effort that could have been made, short of an official treaty, the introduction of smallpox changed everything. But it wasn't simply a matter of recent events driving the Indians.

In fact, memories ran very long in the uppermost Indian circles, with many of the decision-makers well remembering the events of 1962, and China's long-term efforts to act as the leader of the Third World. The competition only grew more heated as both nations entered the Capitalist Way, buying into the American construct of world economics, and independently raising large, powerful middle-classes by toeing the Yankee line. The Chinese resented the Indians' success in taking over the U.S.'s outsourced services; The Indians resented the Chinese for their success in taking over the U.S.'s outsourced manufacturing. Both thirsted for oil, and India deeply resented China's quiet support of Pakistan.

Perhaps it was their hatred of the Chinese, or the smallpox attack, or maybe a leftover allegiance to the West borne out of a century of British Colonialism, or possibly it was the more recent flow of dollars, military technology and investments from their American friends; at any rate, the Chinese were caught completely by surprise.

First, the agreed upon logistical support arranged to be provided by the Indians to the Chinese on their westward March through the Khyber Pass never materialized. Then, after the disastrous fighting in the Persian Gulf, and their humiliating defeat at the hands of the Western armies, when the Chinese returned East, only to find the Khyber pass effectively sealed off by the American atomic bombings, they were unpleasantly greeted with artillery bombardment, ground attack aircraft, and small arms fire.

"For 300 million Indian dead!" came the shouts, down from the mountains, as hell rained upon the returning Chinese.

The Chinese were furious, and those that made it across the high passes from Afghanistan through India and Pakistan, frostbitten, starving and defeated, back into western China, vowed revenge. When they returned, especially when they saw the cities that had been completely destroyed, there was more urgent work to do for what remained of the People's Militia.

Next, there was the matter of revenge against the lying governmental authorities who had promised them ultimate victory. The gown had been rudely stripped away from the chimera, and there were questions that needed answering. Perhaps the answers would be more forthcoming than in the past, especially at the points of what remained of 200,000,000 gun barrels?

Last Out, Bottom Of
The Ninth – Korea

With over a billion dead, an Indian subcontinent reeling from the scourge of a major smallpox epidemic, a China whose cities had been destroyed and whose armies had been defeated, and a world whose systems of trade, energy production and communications had been nearly completely destroyed, the world held its breath in the hopes of a miracle.

A message came from the newly united Korean Republic, in the form of an offer for the immediate cessation of hostilities, with negotiations on a permanent and lasting peace, and a plan for rebuilding, sent via personalized letters couriered by every available pilot that could fly anything navigable to the capitals of the world's nations.

The offers were immediately accepted in Bejing, followed in a rapid torrent by Washington, New Delhi, and the remainder of the civilized world.

The Korean offer had been just what the world needed, and a grateful humanity watched as the leaders of nations gathered to begin what would be, perhaps, the beginning of the end to all wars.

World War Three was coming to a close.

Just Another Chinese Movement

"Who planned on what to do with the People's Militia after the war?!" bellowed the Chinese Premier.

"No one, sir," came the Minister of Defense's timid reply. "We assumed victoriousness."

"Disarm them, immediately! Send them to the cities to begin rebuilding, and clear away the dead."

But the order came too late, as millions of Chinese, armed with nothing more than small arms, made their way back to the Motherland on foot, back over the Himalayas, or by whatever boats they could commandeer, running the Southeast-Asian gantlet and back to the relative safety of south China.

Once having been repatriated, these 'soldiers', angry, disappointed, defeated and disillusioned, marched upon what remained of the biggest cities, looking for answers from the central governmental authorities.

No fewer than 20,000,000 of them rallied around the outskirts of the former Beijing, ignoring the radiation, and the warning shots, and the shoot to kill orders of the People's Liberation Army and Public Security Bureau gendarmes. Within days, the protesters moved first beyond the outer ring of the capitol, and then through the inner rings and on to the ruins of Great Hall of the People, and the Forbidden City.

But the Communist rulers had long earlier fled the city, to fight another day, perhaps, and the end of another great dynasty had arrived, as the People's Militia made revolution, bringing the demands of a newly freed people back home to roost, like a boomerang, at the doorstep of the government.

The scenes repeated themselves in each of China's formerly bustling cities, as returning Militia members joined the sick and dying, and the refugees, and the curious from the countryside, in the first efforts to grasp at the total destruction.

In the days following the lowering of the Red Chinese banners over the middle and smaller cities' governmental posts, an odd series of flags took their place – and the flag which seemed to take popular hold had "Free China" written in red writing, on a blue background, under a white silhouetted map of the Chinese nation.

The newspapers blared daily of newer, more popular democratic movements, and who was in charge wasn't clear, but one thing grew increasingly evident as the weeks and months passed – China was not going to be returning to the days of Communism. Those days had resulted in a lost war, and the loss of face. Now it was time to join the rest of the world in the pursuit of happiness and a state of normalcy.

For the Chinese, it was time to bury the dead, and rebuild.

Aftermaths

Of course, civilization would have to rebuild, but it would be centuries before humankind ever again achieved the global standards of living, exchanges of information, freedom of travel, and quality of life as that which existed before World War Three.

Following the nuclear attacks, there was a period of several years where the weather was cooler than normal, but after that, the trend toward warmer weather continued on for several decades, reflecting the long-term buildup of carbon dioxide in the earth's atmosphere.

Following the war's death and destruction, the earth's population had been reduced by nearly one third, and its energy consumption had been halved. The post-war global conferences which were convened did not focus on energy and global warming, however. Instead, the discussions centered around the immediate humanitarian needs of the survivors, the re-eradication of smallpox, the elimination of all nuclear weapons, and the establishment of treaties outlawing war.

To prevent future wars, it was decided that a global reserve of 100 nuclear devices would be maintained and jointly managed by all of the world's nations, to be used to severely punish any nation that decided to attack another.

To insure the protection of all peoples, a global identification system was established, which tracked all trade, shipments, and traffic, both human and material.

Epilogue

For decades, even the not so prescient had predicted the inevitability of a clash between the rising power that was China, and the undisputed reigning champion of the 20th Century, the United States.

But nobody expects World Wars, and certainly, nobody would have predicted this fight. The Americans still thought like champions. In the back of the typical American's mind, East-Asia was the weakest division in the league, at least militarily. How things had changed. From a post-World War Two high tide, with American power and influence following on the magical drawing forces of the implosion of the Imperial Japanese Empire, the Chinese Civil War, and the failures of the European Powers to re-establish former colonies throughout the region, the tides of history were due to turn, and slowly, they did.

Militarily, the disastrous Vietnam capitulation permanently removed U.S. forces from the Southeast-Asian mainland. Then, Taiwan completely weaned herself from direct U.S. foreign aid, repossessing its U.S. bases, bidding American forces a final farewell. On the Japanese archipelago, Okinawa was returned to Japan by the United States, as the oyabun-koyabun (older-younger brother) relationship between these two former enemies grew less one-sided, and at American urging, the Japanese Self-Defense Forces once again returned to the business of power projection, as befits the world's second strongest economy. Finally, humbled by the force of nature itself, U.S. forces withdrew from The Philippines with a salute from an angry Mt. Pinatubo. The powerful post-World War II U.S. Navy, even briefly rebuilt during the Reagan years, was a 200 ship shadow of its former self. South Korea, with its 30,000 U.S. troops, and Japan, with its significant U.S. Navy bases, were all that remained of the vast former 20th Century East Asian holdings of the U.S. military.

Economically, from the Korean Armistice in the mid-1950s, to the year 2010, East-Asia witnessed the rise of the world's number two economy in Japan, its number three economy in China, its 11th largest economy in South Korea, and the major colonies of the region, the formerly Dutch Taiwan, East-Asia's Boardwalk, with the world's largest holdings of cash reserves, and the British Park Place of the region, and Trojan Horse of Chinese political reform, Hong Kong. In just half a century, the combined economies of the region, benefiting from international trade and American investment, grew to roughly equal the world's largest economy, all the while investing in U.S. issued debt, amassing wealth.

At the end of World War Two, East Asia sorely needed the U.S.; by 2010, the U.S. could not survive as a major power without East Asia.

Let us hope that the delicate balance of power that exists in the region, not in spite of, but inclusive of a rapidly rising China, will assure continued peace, growing prosperity and an appreciation for stability.

DR. TIMOTHY B. DOSEMAGEN

Born and reared in Kenosha Wisconsin, Dr. Tim Dosemagen resides with his family in Southern Arizona. Dr. Dosemagen served in the United States Air Force for 7 years during the Carter and Reagan Administrations as a Cryptologic Analyst, reporting to the National Security Agency. During his 3 years of gathering intelligence in the Republic of Korea, China launched its first submarine launched ballistic missile, while suffering several significant pilot and aircraft defections. Dosemagen was decorated with the Air Force Achievement Medal (1985), the Air Force Commendation Medal (1986), and received the Joint Service Achievement Medal for "...preparing for publication a substantive report of immense benefit within the intelligence community..." conferred in the city of Washington, by Lt. Gen William Odom, DIRNSA, on April 6th, 1987.

After completing full-time government service in 1987, Dosemagen briefly instructed Chinese Mandarin in the Kenosha Unified School District, before joining the professional service of the Boy Scouts of America where he worked for 11 years, finishing as Director of Field Service with the Northeast Illinois Council, based in Highland Park, Illinois. His service area extended from the northern suburbs of Chicago to southeastern Wisconsin, and he served over 18,000 youngsters and 4,000 adult volunteers in 375 local Scout groups.

Dosemagen briefly served as La Leche League International's Director of Operations, and then as Director of Marketing and Funding for the IEF Education Foundation, a California-based organization dedicated to bridging the gap between U.S. educational opportunities and students from China, Taiwan, Korea and East Asia. IEF has offices in Taipei, Taiwan, Washington, D.C. and Shanghai, China. He then served as a consultant to Central Michigan University's innovative College of Distance and Distributed Learning, and then continued his consultancy with the Bright China Management Institute in Beijing. He served as Executive

Director, ABC Child Development, Inc., a $14,000,000 human service agency with a staff of 256 located in El Monte, California. Presently, Dosemagen serves as Director of Academic Affairs with the University of Phoenix's Southern Arizona Campus, and instructs 17 courses in the Graduate School of Business and Management, the Undergraduate School of Business and Management, and the University College, instructing coursework in management, leadership, organizational behavior, international education, critical thinking, employment law and effective written communications.

In addition to his B.A. in Asian Studies (University of Maryland, 1987), Dosemagen holds a Masters in Human Services (Murray State University, 1996), and received his Doctorate in Education – Management of Programs (Nova Southeastern University, 2000).

A Paul Harris Fellow and long time Rotarian, Dosemagen is also a Vigil Honor Member of the Order of the Arrow, an Eagle Scout, an American Legionnaire, was honored by the American Inn of Court of Northern Illinois with its 2000 Distinguished Service Award, serves on the Executive Board of the Tucson, Arizona Council, Boy Scouts of America, and on the Sahuarita School District's Growth and Planning Task Force.

In the spring of 2002, Dosemagen lectured to Chinese educational community consumers in Shanghai and Nanjing, on recent policy changes in United States immigration procedures and post-secondary educational administration, as a result of the terrorist attacks of September 11th, 2001. In the fall of 2004, he lectured in Beijing on leadership and organizational culture, while introducing the teachings of Dr. Peter F. Drucker to Chinese educational consumers. He enjoys writing, translating, traveling, and the great outdoors. His first novel, *Prodigies* (1stBooks, 2003) was quickly followed by a collection of short stories and essays, *The Impossible* (Authorhouse, 2004), and *The Trigger*, (Authorhouse, 2006) is his third work. In 2005, Dosemagen founded *The American Dream Party of the United States of America*, which is expected to field a slate of candidates in the elections of 2016.